A Reading Teacher Teaches Writing

The Reading/Writing Workshop in Eighth Grade

Steve Kelly

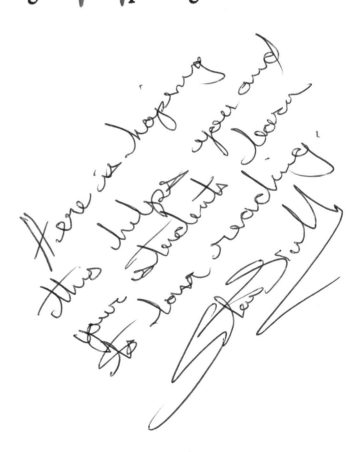

Book Ten: Eighth Grade

Curriculum for Literacy and Implementation Modules

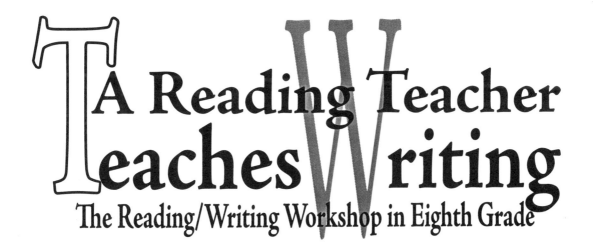

A Reading Teacher Teaches Writing

The Reading/Writing Workshop in Eighth Grade

Steve Kelly

Foreword by
Will Hobbs

Spring, TX ◆ New York

Copyright © 2008 Steve Kelly

All rights reserved. No part of this publication may be
reproduced, transmitted, or stored in an information retrieval system in any form or by any
means, graphic, electronic, or mechanical, including photocopying, taping, and recording
without prior written permission from the publisher.

Library of Congress Control Number: 2008924744

ISBN 978-1-888842-55-5

Printed in the United States of America

Requests for permission to make copies
of any part of the work should be mailed to:

Permissions
Absey & Co. Inc.
23011 Northcrest
Spring, Texas 77389
281.257.2340

Visit us at www.Absey.biz

Dedicated to

Julie, Nicole, and Jarod

# Table of Contents

Foreword

I invite you to visit Steve Kelly's classroom in Weslaco, Texas, in the pages of *A Reading Teacher Teaches Writing*. Sit on one of the couches if you like, at a table, or even on his classroom floor. Dive in to a book full of common sense and proven practices. In between the lines, it's all about the joy of learning. This much I know from my own seventeen years teaching English and reading: if there's no joy, there's very little learning.

It was early in my second career as a full-time writer that I met Dr. Joyce Armstrong Carroll of the New Jersey Writing Project in Texas. Here was a teacher after my own heart. Steve Kelly is another, and there are thousands more across Texas who have rejuvenated their classrooms through the NJWPT. Every time I cross paths with them, I am inspired by their dedication, savvy, work ethic, and love of literature. In an era when language arts teaching has been stunted and repressed in the direction of test preparation, the content and methods of their approach does honor to true teaching, which fully engages a child's intelligence and imagination. As proven time and again, ambitious, expansive teaching is a far more effective way to achieve higher test scores, along with a host of other benefits.

I've seen dynamic and effective teaching across the country, but I've also come across some dead canaries in the coal mine, indicators of how stunted teaching and learning become when narrow-mindedness becomes policy. In tears, a teacher once told me that her district had banned classroom libraries. She actually had to pack hers up and remove it.

I was stunned. Why would they ask so little of their students, of their teachers? Imagine that school district applying the same pedagogy to their baseball teams. Their kids would study baseball all year long without going onto the field and playing the game. It goes against common sense. Those kids would hate baseball and never get any good at it.

Kids often ask me, "Why did you want to be a writer?" It tell them it was simply because I loved reading. It was a case of, "I want to do that!" When I became a teacher, I discovered that the same held true for every one of my students: get them excited about reading, and I had a chance to get them excited about writing.

In Steve Kelly's classroom, you'll find fully integrated reading and writing. Oh, but how I wish I had employed even half of the strategies that Steve Kelly describes for you in his book. My classroom would have been so much more dynamic. My students would have learned much, much more, even in our 45-minute periods. How I envy his 90-minute blocks, which lend themselves ideally to his reading/writing workshop!

Enjoy the photographs of Steve Kelly's students and classroom. Note how much reading and writing his students are doing on a daily basis. Kids are reading class novels--I'm honored that *Downriver* is one of them--and they're reading independently. Significantly, Steve keeps up on young adult literature and is always pitching new books. Teachers like Steve will never get into a rut. They're always looking for the next book, the next new mini-lesson.

Steve Kelly is but one of the fine teachers in the NJWPT tradition. Take a look at their sophisticated yet uncomplicated methods. I found the joy of learning in Steve's classroom, and the joy of teaching as well. May his new book add to yours.

Will Hobbs

Preface

CLAIM: Curricular Literacy and Implementation Modules

In March of 2004, following the NJWPT (now Abydos Learning International) Teachers' and Trainers' Annual Conference, where influential Board of Directors of Abydos Site Directors continued to point out the one gap in the project was implementation, we began work to establish a CO-MISSION of trainers who would represent grades Pre-K through 12. We declared it a "CO" mission, not a "Commission" because we wanted to emphasize its work as one with an equality of purpose.

Invitational letters were sent to fourteen handpicked NJWPT/Abydos Trainers for this important goal. All accepted. With us as directors, we referred to this group as CO-MISSION SIXTEEN. Sixteen of us made it our mission to help young, in-coming, inexperienced teachers and those who loved the institute but who were in a quandary about exactly how to implement it, work it into their stated curricula, or integrate the project's principles, strategies, and philosophy into their day-to-day classroom agenda.

Our initial meeting, held September 4, 2004 at the Hotel Sofitel in Houston, boasted a core group of enthusiastic trainers representing thirteen disparate districts across the state. Since we all agreed our purpose centered on the importance of implementation, we tackled how to research, design, and launch this mission. We asked ourselves: What common sources could we all read? What would be the best way to share our collective expertise? How best could we share our methods of implementation? What title might we use for our work?

After grappling with a host of acronyms ranging from CLIMB: A Curriculum for Literacy Implementation and Model Building to ACCLAIM: A Content Curriculum for Literacy and Implementation Model to our favorite CLIP: A Curriculum Implementation Plan, we dismissed some for negative connotations, others were "taken," still others we felt were not quite on target with our mission, and a few were too cumbersome or wordy. This terrific group of CO-MISSION members finally unanimously chose CLAIM: Curricular Literacy and Implementation Modules.

We liked that the word claim suggested ownership, something we wanted each teacher to experience, grab on to, and hold. We liked the specificity of the words literacy and implementation. We really liked the word modules, suggesting standards, dimensionality, the sense of interchangeability, as well as units of instruction.

We brainstormed and researched and finalized the following sources for all of us to read:

Caine, Renate Nummela and Geoffrey Caine. *Education on the Edge of Possibility.* Alexandria, VA: ASCD, 1997.

Glickman, Carl. "Pretending Not to Know What We Know." *Educational Leadership,* 48 (8) 4-10, 1991.

Hall, Gene E. and Shirley M. Hord. *Implementing Change.* Boston: MA: Allyn & Bacon, 2005.

Jersild, Arthur T. *When Teachers Face Themselves.* NY: Teachers College Press, 1995.

Joyce, B. and Showers, B. "Improving Inservice Training: the Message of Research." *Educational Leadership,* 37 (5), 379-385, 1980.

So we had self-imposed homework to do.

We envisioned a series with a book for each level written by teachers who teach and implement NJWPT/Abydos on that level. We decided to engage colleagues to share in this process through input, feedback, and support. We also wanted to produce videos (still a possibility) so teachers could see implementation in action. To that end, and perhaps ambitiously, we invited a tech expert to our next meeting.

Between 2004 and the first phase of publishing, we met at least once in the summer, several times at the NJWPT/Abydos retreat, and always at the conference. In between these times, cadres met. For example, the Pre-K through first grade met, or the third, fourth, and fifth grades met.

Then we hit our first snag.

The trainer committed to write the twelve grade book moved—not just districts but out of state. We had to find another trainer. Then it happened again. This time the trainer committed to the ninth grade book entered law school. We had to find another trainer. A third trainer became a principal, and although she maintained her commitment, her new position impinged upon her time. A fourth took a position in another district as a curriculum coordinator, but she had worked ahead of time and actually was the first trainer to complete her book.

We were flexible. Deadlines came and went—and we realized our desire to have thirteen books published in one year, thirteen books to be launched at a single conference was not to be. So we regrouped and decided to introduce the books in phases. Phase One, then, would come out in 2008 with subsequent phases in subsequent years.

Throughout the process, we all grew. We listed possible items for the modules—twenty-two to be exact—we discussed the vocabulary of concept, strategy, activity, tactic, and we reviewed levels of lessons. We contacted parents and students for permissions, took pictures, made videos. We studied and contacted authors for Forewords, each of us sharing in the joy when one us received a letter from our "author" agreeing to write a colleague's Foreword. Some even entertained the idea of an Afterword. Most of all we remained cohesive and energized.

So after four years of study, hard work, camaraderie, and lots of writing, we offer you this book of phase one in the series CLAIM: Curricular Literacy and Implementation Modules.

We hope you learn from, through, and because of it. We hope this book and this series helps you make NJWPT/Abydos come as alive in your classroom as it does in ours. We have gained so much professionally and believe we are doubly validated because our work will grow exponentially through you and your students. Know that all lives you touch directly or indirectly will be enhanced because of this undertaking.

May the process be with you......

Joyce Armstrong Carroll, Ed. D., H.L.D. Co-director, NJWPT/Abydos Learning

Series Authors:

Jimmie O'Quinn, Pre-K, Spring Branch ISD
Kim Dumaine, Kindergarten, Richardson ISD
Valerie Sosa, First, Pflugerville ISD
Natalie Hoskins, Second, Friendswood ISD
Robin Johnson, Third, Lovejoy ISD
Bobby Purcell, Fourth, Amarillo ISD
Jodi Hughes, Fifth, Austin ISD
Suzi Lockamy, Sixth, Northside ISD
Michelle Jackson, Seventh, Granbury ISD
Steve Kelly, Eighth, Edinburg ISD
Mona Robinson, Tenth, Pasadena ISD
Dottie Hall, Eleventh, Northside ISD

Introduction

When I first started teaching I was lost, not knowing where to start or how to put lessons together, I relied heavily on the textbook and the textbook's questions to guide my teaching. After the first year of teaching from the book, however, I knew there had to be more to teaching reading. I tried everything but could not find my niche. For a few years I floundered, sticking with some strategies longer than others, asking colleagues and reading journals, trying to find something that made sense and helped the students learn. Finally, I decided to go back to school and get my Masters in Reading; this study opened my eyes, making me wonder what I had been doing to my students for the past four years.

Around that same time I purchased a new dog. As I was studying and learning about reading, I was also learning that all dogs are not the same and need as much attention as children do. I found the similarities between learning a new pedagogy and rearing a new pup to be much the same.

Teaching a Puppy

A few years ago two things in my life changed: I had just begun a Masters of Reading program and had also bought a miniature Schnauzer puppy to replace my deceased dog of eleven years. I did not realize then the similarities between the puppy and me. The puppy was learning some rules about living in my house, and I was learning a new pedagogy for teaching.

Learning a new pedagogy after spending years with an old one is like teaching a puppy to live by your rules after having a well-trained dog for years. With a puppy you have to observe their behaviors and decide how those behaviors fit into your lifestyle. After I figured out what behaviors to allow and what not to allow, I got down to business with the pup and down to business implementing this new pedagogy in my classroom.

I became frustrated after numerous attempts to teach my new puppy to go to the bathroom outside. The feeling got overwhelming at times as I attempted various rewards and punishments to get my puppy to do what I wanted. Sometimes I wondered if the puppy would ever learn. Then I calmed down and realized I had only made a few attempts; the puppy really was

1

quite young, so I thought *maybe it deserves another chance and some more attention*. I kept trying. I'd meet with success for a few days and started to feel great, only to come home to a mess. But eventually the frustration lessened; I knew I could be successful, so I thought less frequently about getting rid of the pup but thought I'd try something different with his training. Besides he was so cute and cuddly, I had become attached to him.

Things started to get better between the two of us for quite a while. Then one day I came home and found the dog with his head in the garbage, trash strewn all over the kitchen floor (your administrator has directed you to teach skills, skills, skills in preparation for the state test). Just when I had gotten comfortable with the puppy, I had to punish him and put him outside for the next few days until I could figure out a solution to this dilemma.

Meanwhile, the puppy found a hole in the fence and ran away. I came home, and he was gone. I looked for him but after a time I gave up. I thought up excuses, *the puppy was too much trouble anyway* or *he would have cost too much in time and effort*. I even started to think it was not too smart to buy a new dog after so many contented years with my old one. My neighbors kept asking about the cute little fella and whether I had found him. I answer in the negative, saying it was for the best. They asked me how my kids were taking it because they saw how much fun they were having with the new puppy. I grumbled and went on with my daily chores and got along even though something kept nagging at me.

A couple of days later I got a phone call and the person on the other end of the line said, "I think I have your dog."

I asked, "How do know it is mine? How do you know I lost a dog?"

"I saw your fliers."

I went to pick up the puppy and was surprised to see how happy he was to see me. When I got home I noticed the puppy still remembered some of the lessons I taught him but needed refreshers on others. I hadn't figured out how to handle the garbage incident but decided to handle that hurdle when I got to it again, if it even came up again. I hoped things would go so well "garbage" would never become an issue again. The puppy got out through the hole in the fence on one other occasion, but he didn't stray far from the house and came back when called.

I saw some dogs in the neighborhood doing simple tricks and also saw some on TV, so I decided to see what my puppy could do. The process began slowly but as the puppy caught on, it took less time for each new trick to be learned. I realized, too, that the neighbor was right about the puppy and my kids—they are crazy about each other and have fun together. The puppy learned to be gentle around the kids, and the kids' motor skills and responsibility grew as fast as the puppy.

I felt I could settle back and relax because most of the hard training was over. The only thing left was consistently enforcing the rules and adding a new trick here and there.

Now whenever I visit the neighbors or a friend's house and they have a dog, I size them up against mine. What does their dog know that mine doesn't? Could I teach my dog to do that? Do I want to teach my dog to do that? I began to get the feeling, though it may have been biased, that my dog was the best in town.

I'm still watching other dogs but none has come along yet that can beat my dog.

Many times we start something new, not knowing where it will take us. The important thing is to learn from the experience and incorporate into our individual schemas what we can. It will not always go smoothly, in fact, there is bound to be trouble. But like training a new puppy, with a little give and take, in the end the relationship will last a lifetime

Philosophy

To me, literacy is a word which describes a whole collection of behaviors, skills, knowledge, processes, and attitudes. It has something to do with our ability to use language in our negotiations with the world. Often these negotiations are motivated by our desires to manipulate the world for our own benefit. Reading and Writing are two linguistic ways of conducting these negotiations. So are talking, listening, reflecting, and a host of other behaviors related to cognition and critical thinking.

Brian Cambourne

Thinking back over my teaching career, one of the things that strikes me is the change for the better that occurred when I started my Masters in Reading. Soon after the first year of classes my style of teaching began to change, and I started to implement new strategies—and the kids responded positively to them. This invigorated me as well as the students, so we both got more out of class. Looking back I now see why. It was because I started to develop a philosophy for teaching, a filter, of sorts, through which I could pass inservice material, lessons from my colleagues, or journal articles on teaching techniques to see if they were going to work in my classroom, with or without a few modifications. Taking classes at the university helped me discover the research out there on techniques and styles of reading instruction, and then I experimented with them, finding the ones that suited both my students and me.

Then a few years ago I realized that the New Jersey Writing Project in Texas (now Abydos Learning) has much the same philosophy about writing that I had adopted and learned about reading, with many of the same resources, authors, and researchers I had already read.

Because it is important for teachers to have a philosophy about teaching, the only way to develop one is to look at the credible research available about instruction and choose what will works best. NJWPT is one of the best ways to study theory and research on writing in a short period of time. In three weeks teachers are introduced to Emig, Calkins, Atwell, Lane, Zinsser, plus many more writing scholars. Following that introduction, teachers may apply to become trainers for another year of intense study.

We, as teachers, need a philosophy and the background to stand and fight for something we know is right for students. When administrative, state, or test pressures becoming wearing, research shows us how and why we are teaching the way we are. Philosophy gives us the ability to know immediately what we need to do and make it work in our classrooms. We know where we were headed; its helps us stay the course when students start to wobble and the whole lesson starts to come off track.

It does take time to develop a good philosophy. It takes time to read and digest information, to plan, to set goals, and to try out the techniques and strategies. But it only takes a taste of something real, like research, to make a teacher hungry to learn more. After that taste, philosophy is set in motion and the living process of a teacher is born.

My philosophy started with an introduction to process as opposed to product, much the same as the introduction at the beginning of the Abydos three-week institute. I started to question the way we were teaching students to read, using skills in isolation, phonics out of context, and worksheets instead of books. None of it seemed to jibe with how I learned to read. We started reading and discussing Brian Cambourne and how he taught students from twenty-six different languages to read in English. He modeled with authentic texts; he followed with discussions were over things the students found meaningful. I realized that this was the way I learned.

During the next two years I read Donald Graves, Regie Routman, Nancy Atwell, and Louise Rosenblatt. In all of these texts and within all this research, the same themes arose—process over product: Figure out what to do as a good model for reading and model it, use authentic instruction over dittos, give students real tasks to work with or discuss, encourage interaction with each other and the text, become a facilitator not a lecturer, and help students learn on their own rather than preaching at them. Students learn 90% of what they themselves have to teach others; only 10% of what they are told.

As I continued my teaching and learning over the next few years, I also continued to read journal articles about teaching trends and techniques. I subscribed to *The Journal of Adolescent and Adult Literacy* and *Educational Leadership*. As I came across interesting teaching ideas, I fit them into my philosophy by bending or mending them to fit my style of facilitating. I also attended workshops and other staff development opportunities and through these I found new authors and researchers to add to my philosophy, such as Barry Lane and Chris Tovani.

One of the most influential workshops I attended was the NJWPT/ Abydos Three-week Summer Writing Institute. I had dodged going to it for years because I was teaching reading not writing, but then I realized that all the research I had been reading stated that reading and writing were inseparable. I also realized that my classroom was based on equal parts of reading and writing, but I was not taking the writing through its full process. So I relented and attended the institute. It ended up reconfirming my philosophy and adding a new component to my teaching arsenal. I became a writing teacher as well as a reading teacher. The philosophies meshed so well and the ways that Carroll and Wilson, Zinsser, Calkins, and Jensen talk about teaching corroborated my own experience teaching. As I studied, I nodded my head in agreement, having ah-hahs. It made me wonder why I had waited so long to take this training.

My classroom is now a rich mixture of reading, interpreting, writing, revising, discussing, and facilitating learning. I continue to learn and incorporate new strategies into my teaching. I doubt I will ever stop. If a strategy does not use authentic literature or if it does not foster a natural process of learning, then it does not get my time and effort. I floundered around for the first couple of years of teaching and thought it was going to be tough going for the rest of my career, but once I found a philosophy to hang on to, to drive what I do in the classroom, I have found teaching to be easy and enjoyable and something I know I'll do until I retire.

A philosophy based on research and data, one with a natural learning process for students, should be flexible and reliable, will never go out of style or out of date because it continually adapts to the ever-changing demands of education and society. A philosophy is not a program that is bought or thrown away because a test changes; it is a core of beliefs backed by research and practice that work to teach students to learn. Nothing more, nothing less—just the simple reality—students learn!

MY BLOCK SCHEDULE
Based on two forty-five minute periods

First Half of Block

twenty minutes of SSR
    (Reading their independently chosen novel)
ten minutes of Journal Writing
    (Either about the novel or not)
fifteen minutes for Minilessons
    (twenty minutes if I use the five minute passing time between classes)

Second Half of Block

forty-five minutes of Reading / Writing Workshop
    Students spend the entire period in one of the following groups, switching daily.

SSR—Sustained silent reading of the class novel
W—Writing as response to the class novel
CND—Class novel discussion
IND—Independent work towards comprehension
JR—Journal writing towards publication

A WEEK'S SCHEDULE

	Mon.	Tues.	Wed.	Thurs.	Fri.
Group One	SSR	W	CND	IND	J
Group Two	W	CND	IND	J	SSR
Grou Three	CND	IND	J	SSR	W
Group Four	IND	J	SSR	W	CND
Group Five	J	SSR	W	CND	IND

NJWPT/
1 Abydos
Essentials

"As students write responses, they, in turn, become authors of meaning about or because of the words that have been shared. This appropriation of meaning and shared ownership is sometimes called writing to learn."

Joyce Armstrong Carroll

During the NJWPT/Abydos Three-week Writing Institute, we were bombarded with a myriad of ideas, theories and strategies—so many it was hard to keep them all straight or even remember what was to be used when. After I had taken the institute, I was overwhelmed with the information and had a hard time figuring out what was integral to the process and where to start. After working with the process and strategies for a year, reading the literature to become a trainer, and facilitating my first summer institute, I realized that there were certain aspects to NJWPT/Abydos that were core to its philosophy, and there were other strategies that facilitated the learning of these core teachings or strategies.

I have categorized the teachings into three lists: Writing Essentials, Share Strategies, and Journal Topics. For me this made sense and helped me to figure out how to get the information across to the students. I use the "Essentials" as the core and make sure that the students understand these concepts, like building blocks, to help facilitate their ability to write. The "Share Strategies" uniquely integrated by NJWPT/Abydos, and as I state later, are key ingredients for helping students understand how they and others write and how to incorporate the strategies they read into their writing. The "Journal Topics" are ways to get the students started, to help them find items to write about that are meaningful to them. Using pieces from all three lists helps me to plan and remember that student learning is based on three tenets, teaching (Writing Essentials), sharing or discussion (Share Strategies), and student engagement (Journal Topics).

The Writing Essentials of NJWPT/Abydos are lessons from the institute that were drawn from many different researchers and theorists. These strategies and processes give depth and meaning to the writing process. It is through these lessons that students learn there is fun and joy in writing, grammar, and punctuation. The unique approaches that are outlined in this book are not the end-all or only one way to teach; they are a starting ground to bring the art of teaching writing back from something that is despised and hated to something that is fun, desired, and satisfying.

Writing Essentials

Reporter's Formula (Carroll & Wilson, *Acts of Teaching: How to Teach Writing*, heretofore referred to simply as *Acts*, 75)

Reading Time

Writing Time

Looping (*Acts*, 74)

Pentad (*Acts*, 76)

Writing Conferences (*Acts*, 174-76)

Classical Invention (Aristotle's Principles, *Acts*, 76-78)

Hexagonal Writing (*Acts*, 79-82)

Ratiocination (*Acts*, 240-45)

Tom Smith called Sarah Lou is here. (*Acts*, 187-88)

Clocking (*Acts*, 282-84)

Genre (*Acts*, 101-03)

Two Arguments, Strawman, etc. (*Acts*, 136-44)

TRIPSQA (*Acts*, 246-61)

The Brain

T-Units (*Acts*, 458-59)

Sentence Combining (*Acts*, 232-34)

One of the essential tenets of the NJWPT/Abydos is providing time **Reading and** for students to read and write. It is important to allow students enough **Writing Time** time to read and see the different ways of putting words together, writing styles, and voices that others use. It is the only way for students to get ideas, build craft, and find their way into becoming a potential author themselves. After they have read and experienced these new ideas, they need time to experiment with them: to try new writing techniques or styles, to attempt to blend them in with their own voice or mix them together to create voice.

I have found that Sustained Silent Reading (SSR) for twenty to forty minutes works best for me in my classroom. I started this many years ago after listening to Stephen Krashen at an in-service. He said that to learn all of the words that a high school senior needs to knows we would have to teach them, "six words per day, 365 days a year, for seventeen years." Further, Krashen (2004) states, "It is by using language, primarily by reading, that people understand the meaning of words." Research indicates that reading independently for as little as ten minutes a day has a significant impact on reading test performance, and reading time in class, in even over as short a period as four months, has a significant impact on reading achievement. After hearing and reading about this, I decided to incorporate reading into my class schedule on a daily basis. I have not been disappointed; I have seen my students reading achievement scores surpass others who do not incorporate SSR in their rooms. I know there is more to learning to interpret reading than just reading the words in a book, but this gives the students the opportunity to try the techniques and strategies that they learn in class through minilessons, discussions, and through their own writing.

Fig. 1.1

After students read, they write in their journals for about ten to fifteen minutes. At the beginning of the year, I give them topics to write about to help them get used to the idea of writing. I split these topics up between interpreting information in the book they are reading and writing about themselves. After a few weeks, I start to incorporate days when they can write about anything they want. Once I see that they do not have problems discovering ideas to write about, I just tell them to write. Many students like to respond to the book they are reading. For example, Michael writes about *The Watsons Go to Birmingham*:

> Bryon and Kenny don't get along even though they are brothers. One day Larry Dunn was picking on Kenny and took his money. Kenny went to get his brother Byron at home. The next day at school Byron walked up to Larry Dunn and started telling him stuff like why are you taking my brothers money? It was kind of funny cause Byron kept slapping Larry Dunn around and Larry Dunn, the bully, didn't do anything. Larry Dunn was afraid of Byron.

Others like to write about themselves or experiences similar to those of the character as Jessica does about her life and the book she is reading, *A Season For Goodbye*:

> The other reason I say I like this book is because it has love in it. It makes me remember about the things in my life that have happened that deal with love. I have been in love, but so many times it turns out that when I actually think I have found the right someone, they don't turn out to be the person I thought. It is nice to know that in some books that it is the same for the main character.

Still others like to write poetry, or short stories, or they just rant. Laura writes about what was on her mind:

> Some guys can get me really angry and I don't like to be angry, so I try not to bother anybody. But there are still those immature little boys that think they are "all that" who will bother anybody. Those people are the ones that I really dislike. I don't get it, why do they have to do that? Even though you don't tell them anything they will find something to make fun of you about. Like you don't have name brand shoes, pants, shirt or your hair looks funny, or you have something on your face, something like that. I can't stand people like that, they make me want to pull my hair out, well first I would pull their hair out then mine.

All the students are given the chance to experiment with writing and develop their voice without the fear of making a mistake or being graded (I assess the journals, but I don't assign a grade on each entry). This is essential in the development of a writer.

I have had administrators say that I am wasting educational time with reading and writing that does not have any grade attached. I have shown them the research and my students' test scores. If I am asked to give a grade for the journals I will give a grade for completion or the act of writing, 100 if they write, 0 when they don't. Depending on administrators and district policies of grading, teachers have to figure out what will work. What is non-negotiable is that the students have that time to read and write.

Reporter's formula is a prewriting technique based on the standard journalistic approach to gathering information—Who? What? Where? When? How? By using the reporter's basic questions, a writer may plumb the depths, uncover the hidden, or startle the unexpected onto the blank page.
—Carroll & Wilson, *Acts of Teaching*

REPORTER'S FORMULA

Reporter's formula is one of the easiest strategies to incorporate into the classroom. Most teachers use it the first day to help learn something about the students and as an introduction to writing. Unfortunately, many teachers stop using it at that point, not realizing the potential it has for understanding characters in a novel. Instead of only having the students interview each other, I have them interview characters. Instead of answering as themselves, I have students answer the questions as the characters in the novels they are reading. I assign different characters to students and pair them up differently so that some of the students are the same character but are paired with other characters. When the students read their end product, the class discusses the differences of the responses they noticed. Also, students discuss the content of the questions and probe different interpretations of the answers. These activities lead to a much deeper understanding of the characters. But before that can be done, enough must be known about the characters for the students to interpret what different characters might say or how they might react. That's when we do reporter's formula.

Steps for Reporter's Formula

1. Distribute three 5x8 inch index cards to each person.
2. Choose partners, preferably one they don't know well. Give 3 minutes.
3. Have them fold two of the cards in half and number them 1,2,3,4 and the unfolded one 5.
4. In section one; have them write 5 questions they want to ask the other person.
   Remind them of the Who, What, Where, When, Why, and How questions. (allot 5 minutes)
5. Have them ask their questions to each other and record their answers in section 2. (allot 7 minutes)
6. Have them circle the one answer they like best and want to know more about. In section 3 they should generate four to six more questions that focus on that answer. (allot 5 minutes)
7. In section 4, record your partner's answers. This time try to capture the exact words and body language. (allot 7 minutes)
8. Use section 5, both sides if necessary, to write a draft based on the answers they recorded. They should try to hook the reader immediately, use quotes and to find an angle. (allot 12 minutes)
9. Read your draft to your partner, who confirms or corrects the facts and points out what they like. (allot 3 minutes)
10. Revise, title, and put your name on the card. (allot 3 minutes)
11. Invite volunteers to share aloud.

This is a good intro activity before a research unit, because it deals with:

Gathering Data
Analyzing Data
Identifying a focus
Synthesizing
Presenting data concisely

Looping

The beauty of looping, a term coined by Peter Elbow (1981, 59), lies in the fact that students experience a prewriting strategy that not only helps them focus but also enables them to find their "centers of gravity," as Elbow calls them (1973,20). These centers pull the students; they are the nuggets nestled within the writing that hold some attraction, a promise that they would be worth writing about.
—Carroll & Wilson, *Acts of Teaching*

I start looping early in the school year. It is important for students to learn how to find and narrow their topics or to figure out just what it is they want to write about. Looping helps students begin to see how they can take any prompt and write about it using their own experience, making it their own. This strategy should not be taught once and left on the shelf but used and reused time and again. I have found that using looping with prompts centered on the setting and plot of a novel helps students delve into their experience and relate better to what is happening in the novel. I start by asking students to write about a specific problem in the book or about one of the main settings. They loop it and see where they end up. As always, we share and discuss connections between the book, the students, and the world.

Pentad

The pentad is an elegantly simple strategy that invites writers to examine an event, a happening, or a piece of literature as if it were a drama with actors, acts, scenes, purposes, and agencies pivoting on human motives and motifs. Adopted from Kenneth Burke's five key terms of dramatism, fully explained in 'The Five Key Terms of Dramatism' (155-162) as well as in his A Grammar of Motives, the pentad turns the elements of the drama into generating principles of questions. By concentrating on one of these five terms, students are free not to have to write everything. What usually emerges is a depth of focus and a blend of one or two of the other elements.
—Carroll & Wilson, *Acts of Teaching*

Besides being a great way to get students to narrow their focus and write about a novel or story, the pentad helps students understand what they can write about in regard to a novel or story. I use the pentad at different times in a novel depending on how the book is written. If it is written with the plot and characterizations at the beginning (frontloaded), I use it early on. If it takes a while for the characters to develop or the plot to become clear, I use it toward the end of the novel. Students need to have enough information to use and combine with their own insights and experiences; they need to be able to focus or hone in on one topic that interests them for the pentad to work effectively. Again, there is the recurring suggestion to use this strategy more than just once throughout the year.

Jessica writes out of the novel *Feeling Sorry For Celia* about "Actors" Who is it?—one of the five writing stances explained by Burke:

Elizabeth is a girl whose life hasn't been all that easy, yet not that hard either. She is not exactly organized and responsible when it comes to school work or at home. She is a messy person because her room is always unclean with her clothes thrown on the floor and lip gloss all over her Mermaid quilt. Elizabeth is not ready to be a teenager and can't take all of the responsibilities that go along with it. At school she doesn't do her homework, the chapter of math or the English essay; she doesn't even bother to try. Elizabeth does not like oatmeal at all, and when her mother gives her some she just ends up feeding it to her dog, Lochie. She has a best friend named Celia whom she seems to care about more than herself. Elizabeth and her mother don't get along very well because there is no communication, only through letters and notes left on the refrigerator. When they do talk face to face they usually end up fighting for some stupid reason. Her interests are mostly running long distances and playing volleyball. Her father left them when she was a little girl and a few months later he got remarried with a lady named Veronica who had a son about her age.

Jessica goes on to use this information later in a well-thought out character analysis paper. When she was first asked to write something about the novel she had just read, she only had few ideas. After I modeled the pentad and invited them to practice writing from one of the stances, she saw where she could go with it.

Burke's Pentad

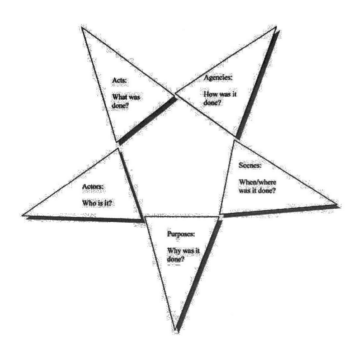

*Writing conferences, which are woven throughout the writing process,
provide a time for teacher and student to discuss a piece of writing.
Conferring demands active listening on the part of both conferees. If,
As Judith Sanders suggests, some 93 percent of what we communicate
is nonverbal, teachers trained in the techniques of the writing conference
attend equally to the nonverbal and verbal language taking place. They
know that tones, expressions, and gestures emerge as significant subtexts of
meaning and can be as important as the words spoken.*
—Carroll & Wilson, *Acts of Teaching*

An integral part of the writing process is the writing conference.
Helping the student to become a better writer is easier for both the
teacher and the student when conferring happens one-on-one. In *How's
it Going?* Carl Anderson explains that the goal of a writing conference
is twofold: first, conversations about the work students are doing as
writers; second, conversations about how the teacher can help students
become better writers. The writing conference is not about trying to
"fix" student writing, it is about how to help students grow as writers.
The teacher's job is to listen and then respond by asking questions that
elicit responses from students. This will help them progress with their
piece. I find that scheduling conferences with each student works best
at the beginning of the year, but as the year progresses, I find that letting
the students schedule their conferences as they need them works best.
Students do not know what to do or say at the beginning of the year
and see no reason for a conference unless they are shown how it can help
them. As the year progresses, they realize they can always come talk, and
I will help them work through their problems or answer questions about
their writing. I require my students to have at least one conference with
me over each finished piece of writing they turn in. Most see me many
more times.

Classical Invention   Classical invention is a strategy that fits well when discussing theme or the message of the novel because it starts with the simple and moves to the more complex. This strategy can be used in a couple of ways. One way is to start at the beginning of the novel with an idea of what the theme or message is and move through the book with the heuristic becoming more complex as more information is read.

Another way of using classical invention is as a culminating activity where the students identify the theme or message in the novel and use the heuristic to guide their writing about it. This is not a strategy that works with all novels; it works best with novels that have an overt, explicit, or stated theme, and it works well with novels that have a variety of well-developed themes or messages. I have found it best to model the process of classical invention first with the class using a short story, then apply it a novel, and finally allow the student to use it on their own with another novel.

Questions for Classical Invention

Definition
What connotations can be applied to this topic? (What does it mean?)
Can this topic be divided into parts?

Comparison
How is the topic similar to other like topics?
To what degree?
How is it different?
To what degree?

Relationship
What causes or caused this topic?
What are its effects?
What came before it?
What are its opposites?

Circumstances
What makes this topic possible?
What would make it impossible?
What are some past facts about this topic?
What are some future predictions about it?

Testimony
Are there any sayings, rules, laws, precedents, or maxims about this topic?
What do credible sources say about it?
Have there been any testimonials about it?

This strategy helps students connect the novel to themselves and the world around them. For those who dislike the standard book report or redundant summaries, I recommend hexagonal writing. By using this strategy, students are better able to write a nicely layered piece. In writing from the six different perspectives, students focus on each one individually for a period of time, so that each section gets the same amount of attention. When they are all brought together, the student's style and voice surface.

Students become creative and work to give the paper an organizational flow when they transition among the perspectives. I model this at the beginning of the year with the novels we read as a class. Once I model and they understand and have internalized it, I use it as a check on their independent reading, assigning it once every six weeks for one of the books they have read. Effective for the students, hexagonal writing helps them delve below the surface into deeper reading and thus deeper comprehension. It is also an effective aid in helping students write meaningful literary pieces versus the mundane book report.

Triangle 1
Plot Summary   Steps and
   What is the plot?   Questions for
   In a couple of sentences explain what the story was about. Hexagonal
    Writing

Triangle 2
Personal Allusion
   How does this story/novel relate to your life?
   Write a memory of something that relates to you or someone else.

Triangle 3
Theme
   What is the message you got after reading the book? Explain.
   Social – a message that applies to society.
   Universal – a message that applies to all people at all times.

Triangle 4
Analyze Literary Devices
   Find and cite examples of the following from the book:

             Similes - a figure of speech that compares two basically unlike things, using words such as *like* or *as*. ("Years hopped along like a tode with arthritis," *Snoring Beauty* by Bruce Hale.)

             Metaphors - a figure of speech that compares unlike things without using words such as *like* or *as*. ("…you will barely see the sky, only small blue puzzle pieces, *The Underneath* by Kathi Appelt.)

Personification - a figure of speech that gives human qualities to an animal, object or idea. ("Sorrow knocked at my door, but I was afraid;" *Spoon River Anthology* by Edgar Lee Masters.)

Imagery—descriptive language that deals with any of the five senses—something that paints a picture in your mind. ("They were both tall and skinny, with tiny mustaches and white beards on just the tips of their chins" *Esperanza Rising* by Pam Munoz Ryan.)

Triangle 5
Literary Allusions

What other literature does it remind you of?

What does it remind you of in terms of other books, movies, or songs?

Triangle 6
Evaluation

What is your opinion of the book?

Did you like it? Why? Why not? Support your answer with evidence.

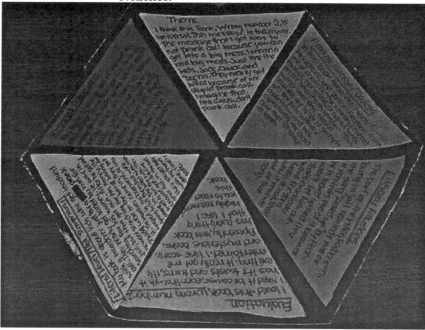

Fig. 1.3

Ratiocination guarantees that students will use:
- *higher-order thinking skills,*
- *revision skills in a context, and*
- *concrete signals to reenter their own writing.*

With ratiocination, teachers find they use some codes, clues, and decodes with every piece of discourse. In time, student writers internalize some clues.

—Carroll & Wilson, *Acts of Teaching*

Ratiocination is one of the best ways I know to get students to look at their writing and analyze three basic things:
- "to be" verbs,
- sentence lengths,
- beginnings or transitions.

The beauty of this strategy is that once students have gone over how it works and what they should do with their papers, they are able to repeat the process on their own when they are ready. After using ratiocination over time, students begin and continue to think more about their verbs as they write, and they vary their sentence beginnings and sentence lengths. The process of ratiocination makes concrete the difficult act of revising for a beginning writer. I personally always have the students ratiocinate for these three aspects and then add others or one of my own from time to time, depending upon what I see as reoccurring problems.

Tom Smith Called Sara Lou is Here

This punctuation strategy can only be done once in the school year. I like to use it to teach the lesson, and then as the year goes on find sentences in the literature that could be ambiguous if the punctuation were different. I also challenge students to come up with sentences or find sentences in their reading that could change in meaning if the punctuation were changed. When they find one, we put it up on an anchor chart and let the other students figure out new forms of the sentence, talking about what the punctuation does for the meaning. Here are some examples of what they have come up with for "Tom Smith called Sarah Lou is here":

Tom Smith called, "Sarah Lou is here."
Tom Smith, called Sarah Lou, is here.
"Tom, Smith," called Sarah, "Lou is here."
Tom Smith (called Sarah Lou) is here.
"Tom … Smith," called Sarah, "Lou is here."
"Tom, "Smith called, "Sarah Lou is here."

CLOCKING

Clocking is a proofreading/editing technique that finds its roots in a brief article "Peer Proofreading" by Irene Payan (124-125). During clocking, students sit facing each other in two concentric circles. This arrangement approximates the face of a clock. The teacher calls out details to be checked. Students in the inner circle remain seated; the other students move one place to the right after each detail is checked. In this way different students proofread each other's work.

—Carroll & Wilson, *Acts of Teaching*

I use this strategy whenever students are ready to publish their work. It is the best editing strategy and takes the least amount of time to get the entire class finished at one time. The students enjoy it because they are not reading the same paper over and over and, in fact, many have found that they don't even have to actually read the paper to do some of the editing. I know they are practicing their skimming and scanning skills. Other students like it because it allows them to read several of their classmates' papers to see how and what they wrote. I like it because by switching papers, students get a fresh focus on the task at hand and eliminate some of the often glossed over mistakes that happen when one person tries to edit for everything on a piece of writing. Whether digital or analog, when clocking is used students enjoy it, if only for the sake of moving out of their regular seating arrangement or in my case out of the classroom into the hallway or library.

GENRE

Genre is something that needs to be taught throughout the year with each literary piece or selection. It is important to introduce the students to as many genres in literature as possible, both through reading and writing. I try to find literature on the same topic but written in different genres. This shows students how messages change or how the information changes to fit the genre. It is important to discuss the components that make each genre unique as the students try them. I present a minilesson on the specific genre before we start and I show examples. Once we have read for a while and students have been given the opportunity to read some other examples, I challenge them to try writing a piece in that genre. The products are often surprising to both the student and me. Teaching genre not only helps students develop voice, it also develops the students' appreciation of the voice of others.

BRUFFEE'S ORGANIZATIONAL PATTERNS

Kenneth A Bruffee in A Short Course in Writing gives detailed forms for the writing done by students. He says, "The purpose of this book is to provide a new model for learning the principles of discursive writing." The writing exercises allow for "freedom of subject matter and opinion, but limits their form of presentation" and are worth some consideration. When the forms are taught as a natural outgrowth of what the writer

*has to say, rather than as an imposed form, then deeper understanding of
organization occurs.*
—Carroll & Wilson, *Acts of Teaching*

	Two Reasons

Introduction with Proposition at the end

First reason developed
Explanation or defense

Second reason developed

	Nestorian Order

Introduction with Proposition

Second best reason developed
Minor reasons

Major reason developed

	Strawman and One Reason

Introduction with Proposition at the end

Main opposing argument
Refute the opposition

Major positive reason developed

	Concession

Introduction with Proposition

Important opposing argument

Concession
Positive argument developed

These organizational patterns are essential for helping students write a persuasive paper. It may seem that this would be covered only once during the year, but I have found the topics of young adult fiction lend themselves to persuasive writing, and students are eager to voice their opinions on controversial subjects. Therefore I make anchor charts of these four patterns and keep them up for the entire year because many times throughout the year students ask clarifying questions about what one pattern has that another does not. I do not have to assign a persuasive paper for many of my students to want to write them. They are motivated by what we discussed about the novel. These patterns have brought the persuasive paper back to something I enjoy reading better than the old repetitive papers of, "Because I think so" or "In my opinion." The students like them because they provide structure for their thoughts and make them think about both sides of an issue.

In the following excerpt from Fabiola's persuasive paper over an independent novel she read, she decided to use "Two Reasons" as her organizational pattern. She developed two reasons for her position and then one against. The reason against her argument was weak so she decided not to even use it in the development of her paper. I believe the topic of the paper will tell you why.

> Sex, what is the first thing you think about when you hear that word? Now think, what do teens think about when they hear it? Would you like your son or daughter to be having sex at such a young age? Of course not, who would want their daughter to get pregnant? Like all of your parents, I agree, teenagers should not be having sex.
>
> One of my main reasons that I think teenagers should not have sex is that the girl can become pregnant. If that girl is your daughter you are not going to be too happy!

Fabiola went on to elaborate, stating that her other reason was the possibility of catching a sexually transmitted disease. She also ended her piece with a very strong conclusion. The students tackle complex and controversial topics with these organizational patterns, these patterns help them to find a focus and see the topic from other perspectives.

TRIPSQA   *One way to help students understand the flexibility of paragraphing is to use the two paragraph patterns identified by Alton Becker in his article "A Tagmemic Approach to Paragraph Analysis." TRI is the first pattern; PS/QA is the second.*

The acronym TRI stands for the traditional Topic, Restatement, Illustration pattern. When using this pattern, the writer states a topic, extends the topic, and uses examples to support that topic. After learning this traditional pattern, students working in groups may brainstorm permutations, for example, TIR, TII, ITR, and TRIT. After brainstorming, they may use these permutations to analyze their writing.

The acronym PS/QA stands for Problem/Solution and Question/Answer. These may, in fact, take up many sentences or may be shaped into paragraph blocks.

—Carroll & Wilson, Acts of Teaching

A strategy that definitely belongs at the beginning of the year, TRIPSQA helps the students with internal coherence. This is a definite building block that many of my students need several times over the first six weeks. Using a variety of concrete manipulatives, some edible and others not, I make sure to have some bagged up and ready for anytime the students start to write. I have found that once I have taught TRIPSQA, students want to do it on their own when they begin revising or when they feel that they have gotten lost in their writing. I keep several bags of the manipulatives, the non-edible ones, on hand at a writing center.

The Brain

Even though I do not teach psychology or biology, I do have a degree in psychology. I have always found it important to teach my students how their brain processes information and some cues or tricks to help their brains remember things. I have found that explaining short and long term memory, for example, helps students become better readers, especially those students who once said, "I read but after a while I forget what was at the beginning." I teach them visualization and rereading strategies after I explain how their memory systems work. Keeping current on brain research also helps me to modify my teaching techniques and maximize students' potential and creativity.

T-Units

A third means of measuring students' growth is through the descriptor coined by Kellogg W. Hunt. The T-Unit measures student's syntactic maturity, that is, their ability to write sentences with sophisticated levels of thought. Hunt defines his descriptor as "a single main clause (independent clause) plus whatever clauses and nonclauses are attached or embedded within that one main clause" (92). It is "the shortest grammatically complete unit that is not a fragment. The T stands for "terminable." Simply stated, a T-Unit is a single main clause and whatever goes with it" (93).
—Carroll & Wilson, *Acts of Teaching*

At the beginning of the year I teach T-Units to help the students get over their short, choppy sentences from a summer of no writing. Students can and will be able to join some of their shorter sentences together even though they do not fully understand the clauses, phrases, and punctuation they need to use to combine them. I teach T-Units again after the long Christmas break, as a reminder and an introduction into phrases and clauses. Throughout the year I ask students to count the T-Units in their paragraphs to see how they are progressing. I explain information about sentence maturity and we look at examples of long complex sentences from literature, discussing the reason the author decided to write that way as opposed to a series of shorter sentences. I find that students like to take long compound/complex sentences apart to see how many T-Units there are, and that takes as much skill as putting them all together in the first place. Bottom line, T-Units help bring about more mature sentence construction and better, more complete thoughts.

These techniques and strategies are not static. They are continually in use by the students as they write daily. As the teacher, I have to evaluate and recognize when our class needs a refresher on one or more of the strategies and provide an appropriate minilesson. Monitoring writing through conferencing and reading their work is as much a part of teaching as standing in the front of the room and modeling how to do something. Giving the students time to try the strategies and the opportunity to take risks and make mistakes helps them to become better writers. I just have to show them what to try once in a while, but that is what NJWPT/Abydos is all about—modeling and discussing different ways to make students better writers.

2 Share Strategies

Share sessions serve as public, teacher-supported conferences. By participating in them, students learn how to confer with each other in one-to-one peer conferences.

—Lucy Calkins

The share strategies are to NJWPT/Abydos what punctuation is to writing. As I went through the institute, I felt out of my element when it came to writing for publication. The share strategies helped me overcome my fears and helped me realize I was a good writer with good ideas. As a teacher, I have seen the same thing happen to students; they are reluctant to try at first but after the first sharing they gain momentum and eventually volunteer to read to the whole group.

The share process is important to the choosing of a piece of writing as well as to its development. A stage of the writing process that is not always stated and often overlooked, sharing ideas offered freely are not only critiques of each other's writing but ideas about craft. As students listen, they hear how words are put together and how different ways of saying something can create a mood or picture. These difficult concepts would not have been noticed had they not been shared or if students were not closely listening to other students' experiences.

I have found that students are reluctant to write and share for fear of being put down. After a few share sessions, which I monitor, students become comfortable with sharing. The students eventually start to act like teachers or facilitators in their share groups and I hear comments such as, "you should try this…" or "I like this part but I am confused by …" comments that make the writer think and re-enter his or her writing. By the end of the year, students are less fearful about writing an essay or anything for any teacher. The only complaint I hear is that in other classes they are not allowed to share and group together to hear other ideas or get feedback. I always tell them that they know how to do it, so they could do it on their own time with others from their class.

SHARE STRATEGIES

Pointing   Four to five students per group. Each student jots down words, phrases, images as each group member reads, pointing out what they liked (*Acts*, 151-52).

Pointing is an easy strategy with which to begin. It gets students used to working in groups and sharing their writing. There is no pressure and no criticism, only positive comments about the writing. This strategy makes students feel good; like they have accomplished something. At times I have to remind a few that they are pointing out good things, not critiquing the paper. I spend time in each of the groups and try to listen to one paper being read all the way through and the comments made about it, making sure the process is moving smoothly in each group.

Showing   Four students per group. Each student jots down a metaphor or creates a drawing that comes to mind as they listen to each group member, then they share the metaphor or drawing and explain it (*Acts*, 152).

With showing I begin with a minilesson on metaphors so students have a model and know my expectations. I use this strategy after the students have become familiar and comfortable with sharing because this strategy also helps me teach and check the concept of a metaphor, plus it gives the writer feedback. Students may draw a quick sketch as they listen, but I have found that there usually isn't enough time for them to do that if they are not used to doodling already. The first time I use this strategy, I have the students create a metaphor and explain it. Usually, there are two types of discussion that ensue after a paper is read
  + about the paper,
  + what their metaphors meant.
     At times the talk about the metaphors goes on longer than the talk about the papers, which helps cement the knowledge of what a metaphor is and does.

Telling   Five to six students per group. Each student sketches an EKG reading of the story. Then they tell what the instrument recorded. (*Acts*, 152-53)

I like to use this share strategy when the writing assignment was something that had either lots of emotion or lots of action. It is hard for students to sketch an EKG reading of a paper over the theme of a book. It is much easier to sketch one from a personal experience they had that is similar to the main characters. This strategy gives the writer excellent feedback on the plot of their story and whether they have gotten their message across. Many times students find what they thought they were getting across and what came across don't match. They then have to make a decision concerning which direction to take their paper from there. This is one of those strategies that can be used early on in the year and many times throughout the year.

Summarizing

Five students per group. Each student writes the main idea, summarizes the main idea in one word, gives a synonym, and then each shares (*Acts*, 153).

I like this share strategy because it helps students understand that a summary does not include every little detail. Inviting students to summarize the paper they heard in one word and then explain what they meant helps them become concise. The synonym helps the students learn about the multiple meanings of words and how words are connected to each other; it helps with vocabulary. Students learn how different people connect words, their style, and how people think—all of which affects the meaning of words, all adds to their knowledge of what that word means. The writer receives feedback on what words they put together means to others and compares that to their intent, hoping to find some common ground.

Analytic Talk

Five students per group. As a peer reads, listeners ask themselves the following questions. Did I like the opening? Was the opening clear and interesting? Would I continue reading if I read the opener in a magazine? Was there a lazy or phony question? After hearing the beginning, am I sure what the writing is about? Did I ever get lost during the reading? Where? Did I ever get confused? Where? Was I left hanging at the end? Was it intentional and effective? (*Acts*, 157-58)

Analytic talk provides students with a first-hand look at which part of a piece of writing matters most to the reader. I usually preface this share strategy with a minilesson on audience, helping the students understand that they may be writing their thoughts, but the reader has to make sense of them and many times what they write and how it reads are two different things. The questions are specific enough to get responses from the listeners yet open enough to lend themselves to interpretation and discussion. Writers often find out that meaning depends upon the listeners' experiences, whether they get the message the way the writer intended or not. This is another share strategy I use early and often throughout the year.

Plus and Minus   Ten students per group. They use the chart on page 155 of *Acts of Teaching*. Members signal thumbs up or down after each reading (*Acts*, 153-54).

Much like analytical talk, plus and minus helps the writer see the readers' interpretation of their words. The difference is in the specificity of the categories the listeners are looking for and the way in which they signal their acquiescence. This share process invites little discussion after the reading, but the thumbs up or down are tallied for each category so the writer literally sees how the audience views or understands their piece. I like to use this share strategy towards the end of the writing process, much like clocking and ratiocination, as one more tool for revising for a final edit. To get through this strategy in the allotted time of a class period, it is often necessary to lower the number of students in a group from ten to maybe five or six.

Large Group   Volunteers share their ideas, concepts, purposes, and audience. Group responds informally (*Acts*, 154-56).

Since sharing with a large group intimidates students, I do not use this share strategy until later in the year, usually after the first semester when the students have had a chance to be in a group with everyone in the class. I usually begin a writing assignment using this share strategy by brainstorming ideas for writing topics early in the writing or prewriting stages, to prepare students to tackle larger or more complex forms of writing. Since it's collaborative, the writer who shares has to be prepared for things to go in any direction; after all they are asking the class for their ideas. In the true sense of a large group share, the students read part of their papers and ask for advice or they share their ideas for a paper. I judiciously limit this share to a few times a year due to the intimidation factor.

Process   Seven students per group. They discuss the following: What problems have you encountered? How did you go about solving them? Have you made any changes? What were they? What prompted them? What are you planning to do next? What help do you need from this group? (*Acts*, 156-57)

This share strategy is different from the others because writers do not actually read their writing. Instead, they talk about their processes and how their papers are coming along; they also ask for help or suggestions where they may need it.

Students first need to know or learn how to talk about the process of writing, and after a few class discussions and modeling of my own writing, they talk about theirs. This gives us a shared language. I use this share strategy early in the year but not as one of the first few. I allow students time to see and experience the writing process, and then I have them try it out. The first couple of times students don't usually know what to say about their writing, but as the year goes on they develop a vocabulary and understand how this level of talk is necessary in the development of a good piece of writing. I use it in the middle of their writing process as a check to see where they are and what direction they think they are going.

Say Back

Four to five students per group. Each student jots down what they liked and what they want to know more about, then they "Say back" what they wrote (*Acts*, 157).

This is an effective share strategy for the beginning of the year, it is non-threatening and helps students learn to say something positive about each other's papers. It also helps students in groups become better listeners because they have to "say back" what they liked. The writer gets to hear what the listeners liked about their piece and what they need to focus on, or they get suggestions based on what the listeners want to learn more about. This works well in groups of four, not so large that the discussion of each paper lacks time to develop. I use this over and over at the beginning of the year to help build rapport among students in new groups.

Highlighting

Four to five students per group. Each student jots down the images they liked. They repeat the images as the writer highlights them on their paper (*Acts*, 154).

This share strategy works wonderfully in conjunction with minilessons on imagery or adding details to writing. Having the listeners jot down images that they liked when they heard the paper and having the writer highlight them so they can see where they are in their paper helps the reader and the writer get a clearer picture of the importance of details in a piece of writing. It also helps the students see, as all of these strategies do, how different people use imagery and how different students have differing styles of writing. The student struggling with imagery is going to get two or three different examples from each of four to five students in the class, plus an explanation of why people liked them. This strategy works better with papers that are geared toward imagery: narratives, short stories or personal experiences.

Double Dyad

Two students per group. They use the preparing for publication chart on page 161 of *Acts*. They read the paper and mark the chart accordingly, then they switch with another dyad and repeat the process with a new partner. (*Acts*, 161)

As with plus and minus, I introduce this share strategy at or near the end of the writing process. Using the "preparing for publication" chart in *Acts of Teaching* (161), students look at the criteria and rate the paper

Conferencing they are listening to, giving the author feedback on how the information came across. Whereas plus and minus can be used at any time during the writing process, I use this one just before publication as a last check of minor errors or as a way for students to discover how their papers are received. I do not use plus and minus, analytic talk, or double dyads on the same piece of writing the students are doing, I mix them up for variety with different pieces of writing throughout the year.

Fig. 2.1

Because it is difficult for students to share, an environment needs to be in place, one that nurtures students and builds a community culture, one that invites sharing and productive feedback. I have found that it is best to start small, with dyads or triads, to encourage reluctant students and get them used to reading to others. Once a minilesson on the rules of sharing have been covered, perhaps anchored on a chart, then it is just a matter of monitoring and debriefing after the share sessions. It is important to provide a rationale and validation for students so they see how listening to others helps their own writing. Modeling and giving positive examples allows them to see that I am paying attention to them and that what they do is valued.

The following are a few of my ideas and comments about the share strategies. There are others, or these may be modified to suit the needs of any classroom. The important thing is to give students time to share in class because it does take time.

Fig 2.2

Some share strategies work better with certain genres of writing. As I became more familiar with them, I saw how each stimulates and enhances a student's ability to be creative and how students feed off of each other to produce better pieces of writing. Remember, like anything new, share strategies take modeling and time. Keep working and modifying. In the end the benefits will prove worth it.

Another benefit to the share strategies is that they allow students to see how others pick information out of a piece of literature and utilize it in their writing. It helps them to get a different perspective of how literature may be dissected and experienced. Next to actual discussions, these share strategies promote comprehension and illuminate how there is no right answer to an open-ended question. It all depends on the experiences of the reader, how they interpret the information, and how compelling is the evidence given as support. This is learned only when that reader shares his or her interpretation through discussion or through the share strategies.

3 Journal Strategies

Journals provide a nonthreatening place to explore learnings, feelings, happenings, and language through writing.
—Regie Routman

Essential to writing is having something to write about—enter—the journal. During the summer institute we were exposed daily to new strategies to get us to think of things to write about. These strategies help jog the memory or force the mind to think instead of sitting idle, drawing a blank, or spending too much time with excuses. Students need to see that writing may emerge from anything—any thought, any discussion, any picture, or any idea. They also need to see that what a person begins to write about often changes dramatically as the mind starts to meander. Journal strategies or idea starters engage the mind and let each writer take off in a way that suits their style.

I have divided journal strategies into three categories: those that take time and preparation, those that are prewriting, and those that are fast and easy to use at anytime. Starting with those strategies that take some preparation, I give some suggestions on how these may be used or what has resulted from their use in my classroom. These are not the only ones that may be used to get students writing on a daily basis, but they are some excellent starting points for all students, especially for students that are reluctant to write or take a long time figuring out what to write about.

JOURNAL STRATEGIES

FreeWriting   Write freely about whatever comes to mind, get down the thoughts as fast as possible without regard to mechanics and rules at this time (10-15 minutes) (*Acts*, 66).

This journal strategy promotes fluency. Some students struggle a little the first few times they do it, but, as the year progresses, they start to pour their thoughts on the paper. They begin to understand the power of not worrying about anything but putting words on paper and getting the thoughts out of their heads. I notice that those students who write copiously during freewriting usually have no problem getting to work when a writing assignment is given. Students who write hesitantly, or have trouble getting the words out of their head and onto paper, benefit most from this strategy. It helps to free students of the thought that they are doing something wrong because then they constantly monitor their writing for mistakes instead of just putting down their thoughts. This is a good strategy to show the important step in the writing process, getting ideas on paper.

Wet Ink Writing

One to two minute bursts of writing what comes to mind, "before the ink dries on the paper." If nothing comes to mind then write, "I can't think of anything" over and over until something does (*Acts*, 66-67).

Much like freewriting, but taking less time—a mere one to two minutes—wet ink writing is a great writing nudge. I usually do not attempt this with my kids until they feel comfortable with writing. Many times kids do not have something they can write about off the top of their heads and it takes them a couple of minutes to get started. Using this strategy they are told to write, "I can't think of anything" over and over again until something does come to mind. This is a useful hint because the brain does not tolerate boredom and will come up with something. This journal strategy really puts a premium on fluency and gets the students' thoughts onto the paper as fast as possible, leaving room for more writing if the student chooses. Related to sentence stubs, it is like an extended prompt that students may tap later.

Trigger Words

Use a carefully chosen word to jog the memory and make connections (*Acts*, 67).

Free Association

When using this strategy the teachers sets up words in a way that invites a double-level connection, Ex: Old _____ Shop   The word that fits in the middle should work at the end of the first word and at the beginning of the second. For example: Old *Furniture//Furniture* Shop. (*Acts*, 67-68)

This journal strategy invites analogies. Students figure out what word would go best in-between two other words, but it has to make sense with both words. Ex: Old _____ Shop. A word that fits in the blank could be shoe, old shoe and shoe shop. This strategy obviously takes some time setting up the pairs of words and thus takes away spontaneity. It does spark some topics for writing and it does fit into the prewriting stage, but I feel it does a better job of teaching vocabulary and multiple meanings of words when a discussion follows. I follow the discussion with a writing time about anything that piqued interest during the class. I use this a couple of times a year and have found that students like to come up with their own pairings, which I use the next time or the following year.

Invisible Writing   Use carbon paper and skewers. Students write to fill the page. This prevents them from rereading what they have already written and promotes deeper thinking.

This strategy does not take much time. It is a fantastic way of getting students to think deeper on a subject and learn to trust their mind instead of constantly looking back and rereading what they have written. The same can be done on the computer by having them turn off the monitor after starting the word processor. This strategy helps students see that their minds continue to think about something and come up with ideas. It helps students eliminate the need to constantly reread what they have written. Instead, they write about *a* topic. I use this as often as I can at the beginning of the year to promote fluency without worrying about mechanics, spelling and punctuation just yet.

Sentence Stubs   Open-ended sentence fragments meant to spark interest and more writing. Ex: Once I thought I would … or I wish I knew … (*Acts*, 70).

Sentence stubs do take a little bit of preparation. Students write ideas for open-ended sentence starters on sentence strips, and I hang them on the wall. Once this is done, the students always have readily available subjects to write about when asked to write. All they have to do is look at the walls. I use this more as a fall back plan rather than actually assigning them a topic. There are times when I ask them to choose one of the sentence stubs on the wall to write about. There are also times I use one of the sentence stubs to write about and model a minilesson. Though I do not assign it to the students as a stand-alone assignment, I use sentence stubs, and students like to have them visible as a safety net of sorts.

Listing   Taking a general topic, students list all of the associations that come to mind. Then they reread the list to see what other ideas or lists come to mind (*Acts*, 72).

When listing, students write associations to a topic and then read these associations and add more ideas, thereby creating a subsequent lists. From this second list, students choose a topic and start to write. I connect this strategy to issues within a novel to help the students focus on something that interests them but at the same time stay with the novel. This also helps bring out different points of view and complexities on an issue that others may not have thought about. The key is to get students to list at least twice, once from the assigned topic and again from one of the topics they come up with on their own, thus fostering personal preference. I use this when I want students to delve deeper into a subject, to get beyond surface ideas.

Blue Printing

Draw the floor plan to your house and then start in one room and write about something that happened there (*Acts*, 72-73).

This journal strategy takes time when first introduced, but from then on students use their floor plans to generate numerous additional topics. It is a good idea to encourage students to really do a good job of drawing their floor plans, even furniture. The more detailed the drawings, the more students remember when they pull those floor plans out later to write out of them or think about them again. I have found that there are so many memories students come up with as they draw the floor plans, they cannot possibly write about them all. The first year I implemented this strategy, I had students pick one memory to write about, but the next time I asked them to write from their blueprints, some students had a hard time remembering what they had thought about when they drew them. So the following year, they added memory starters *as* they thought of them *while* they were drawing. As they drew and thought of something, they would turn the paper over and jot down a sentence to remind them later of what to write about. Blueprinting resembles Paula Brock's "Quick List" with its ready list of topics for students based on their experiences and memories.

Writing Roulette

Each student starts a story and then after a couple of minutes they pass the story on to the next person who reads it and then continues the story; this is repeated several times (*Acts*, 69).

This is one journal strategy that students request again and again. Starting a story and then passing it off to others to add to or complete is both fun and a great way to get reluctant students to try new things in relative anonymity. Many times the stories they receive are not in the style or genre they are used to reading or writing, so they are forced to try something they normally would not. It is also fun for young authors to see how others take their ideas and twist them into products that are far from what they envisioned. I was reluctant to use this strategy for writing because I did not think it was real writing. I was wrong about its benefits. I used it more often with one class of struggling writers and found that soon their fluency and creativity increased and rivaled another class I felt was doing well. Also it contributes to fluency and has the added benefit of fostering creativity. Students try to create parts in the story that are funny or engaging or mysterious. They try not to follow the status quo, but try to take risks or add detail and imagery that will make the next person laugh or want to add more. I try to use this a couple of times during the six weeks, as a break after testing or the completion of a novel.

Brainstorming   Given a topic of interest, students brainstorm as many things as they can about that topic. Usually the ones at the end of the list are more creative (*Acts*, 72).

Like listing, brainstorming helps students come up with a topic to write about. It has been around for a long time and most teachers use it in their classrooms. The key to brainstorming is waiting, waiting for the ideas at the end of the list. Too many times teachers give up on students because it takes too long between responses. But as brain research shows, the deeper the connection, the longer it takes to arrive at its conclusion (Jensen, 1998). The ideas at the end of a brainstorm list are those that are tenuously connected to the original topic or are connected more creatively, and therefore take longer. Don't give up on them too early.

Dialogue   Students take a topic and generate a conversation between two people about that topic (*Acts*, 74).

Dialogue is like writing roulette written by one person. Students like this strategy because they enjoy creating dialogue between two or three people. During a minilesson, I distinguish between dialogue and slangy letter writing. Without that distinction their dialogues look like a letter to a personal friend. Without the minilesson and modeling, students do not know the proper way to paragraph or punctuate their dialogue. This is a fun, easy, and productive way to get students to work on the syntax of dialogue and teach them how writing dialogue is about writing out the important things in a conversation—not everything. Through the use of this strategy, students use dialogue more often in their writing because they are no longer afraid of it. They understand it and realize the potential it has in their writing.

Fig. 3.1

It is important to remember that if we want our students to write deeply and emotionally, we can not expect them to hand in their journals every week. When I want to check on the writing in their journals, I ask them to mark one or two entries and paper clip all of the others together, so I may quickly flip right to the page they intend for me to read. I tell them they need to trust I will not snoop into the rest of their journal, and I don't. I have also checked their journal in conference by sometimes inviting them to read then.

The journal becomes a sacred thing to the students by the end of the year; they carry it everywhere and do not want to leave it in the classroom. I have found that modeling the behavior of jotting down ideas outside of class helps students realize that they may use their journal somewhere other than school. I explain that most ideas come when we are not at school but from where we do the most living. Getting students to write for more than just daily prompts takes time and lots of modeling, but it is well worth it when you see the benefit in a finished piece of writing.

4 Teaching the Novel

As Reading and Writing teachers we share the best literature and writing of the professionals and of our students, guiding them through the process of recognizing the similarities and differences, the qualities that make the pieces good, the books effective. We offer kids options—topics of their choice, books they like, and varied ways of presenting what they know.

—Linda Rief

Finding the right book to read with a class is a daunting task. What will interest them? Will the book be a good example of literature and writing? Does it follow the curriculum? How do I find good books? The most productive way for me to find good books for my students is to read many books. When the students read during SSR, I read along with them. I get lists of best books from the American Library Association, find ones that sound interesting, and start to read my way through the list. I take recommendations from other people, my librarian especially, and I frequently comb the shelves of my school library. After all, those are the books the kids are going to read. As I read, I make mental notes about the author's style and about examples of certain writing skills (although when I hit a really good book, those mental notes take a back seat, and I am totally into finding out the resolution of the book). Those are usually the books that make my "short list." If the book totally consumes me, I am sure it will do the same for most of my students.

When looking for books to read with a class, I take into account certain things. One is the theme or message of the book and another is what writing skills or examples I can pull from it. In the eighth grade I prefer to help students through some of the concerns and issues they face as teenagers. I look for books with characters that are close to their age with realistic problems. I read to see what the character does about the problem and whether that solution is viable for my students. I also look for themes that help teach life lessons, lessons about getting along with others, or lessons concerning relationships in today's society because much of what we do depends upon how we work with others.

I always recommend that teachers look for the way the characters interact with one another and the world around them. Try to choose books that will pique the students' interests and deal with sensitive issues in different ways. Allow books to do some of the values teaching in your classroom. Don't always be quick to mark a book off the list because it deals with an issue in a less than positive light. Often this develops into a good point of discussion and brings out many positive feelings through further interpretation or research. Many times it is the unconventional, yet interesting or unique, approach that hits the target best. I am never afraid to raise some controversial issues that students will be dealing with later in their lives, and I remain prepared to deal with them if they come up. I look at books as a way for students to connect their life and experiences to those of others and learn from those experiences as they read and respond through writing. Using a novel in the classroom provides coping strategies or at least coping options.

Another area I look at as I read is the contribution the novel makes to writing as a craft. What has the author done to exemplify the craft of writing? Are there examples of metaphors? Does it have great description? Is there attention to detail? Authors have different styles, providing a rich mix of style and tone. Students analyze how writing the same message may be done differently. Once I find an author who shows style, metaphor, detail, and so forth, I point out these elements to students, letting them know they will most likely find a consistency of style in other books by that same author. It is important that students learn that there is a purpose in the way an author writes and that the skills we teach them are really used by real people.

I also look for good read-alouds. When I find one, I break it down into the elements of a narrative: characters, settings, and plot. From there I am able to look at specifics about each category and delve deeper into them. To move from reading and teaching a novel, into workshop and using NJWPT/Abydos, I tap the strategies I learned during the summer institute and categorize them.

I divided these strategies into three types: NJWPT/Abydos Essentials, Journal Strategies, and Share Strategies, all discussed previously. Of these three, the "essentials" are the heart of knowing and comprehending whereas the other two are ways to help practice or use the knowledge built through the "essentials." Examining the "essentials," I realized that they all deal with writing, so I decided it became a matter of figuring out where that writing best leads the student. Each "essential" could be used for characterization, plot, or setting. The categories I use may not seem appropriate for everyone, like so many things in the field of teaching, interpretation is the key to implementation.

**CATEGORIZED
ESSENTIALS**

**For Character
Study**

Reporter's Formula
Pentad
Classical Invention
Genre
Organizational Patterns
TRIPSQA

For Plot Study

Looping
Classical Invention
Hexagonal Writing
Organizational Patterns
TRIPSQA
T-Units

**For Setting
Study**

Looping
Pentad
Genre
TRIPSQA
T-Units

Once these are organized and my class and I have our list and understand each strategy, I read through the novel a second time. I use my "Workshop Set Up for a Novel" sheet to plot where each strategy fits. When teachers have done this once or twice for a couple of novels, it becomes unnecessary to refer back to the list; the mind fills with ideas and methods and as we read they just pop into place.

Workshop Set Up
For a Novel

Assignments

Character
　Main
　Minor
　　　　Attitude
　　　　Reactions to others _____
Setting
　Time
　Place _____
Plot
　Problems
　　　　Major
　　　　Minor _____
Mood
　Feeling
　How was it done? _____
Character
　　Thoughts and opinions
　Character Traits _____
Plot
　Solutions
　　　　Who
　　　　How _____
Setting
　　Culture
　Values _____
Plot
　Conflict
　　　　External
　　　　Internal _____
　Resolution
Mood
　Feeling
　How was it done? _____
Tone
　Author's attitude
　Author's ideas
　Opposition _____

To help with organizing information and to add some variety to the writing of information, there are several 3-D graphic organizers that are part of NJWPT/Abydos training. I have listed several along with some ideas of how they may be used, but again, each one may be used to further study plot, character, or setting. It is truly up to the imagination and goals of the teacher about how to use these and for what reason. Teachers may find that using them as I have them listed is fine the first time, but later in the year they often decide that the same 3-D organizer would be great for something entirely different. Creativity and imagination are not only an asset in teaching but also a requirement to keep students engaged. The more ways we find to implement a strategy, the better off our students.

PROJECTS AND 3-D ORGANIZERS	

Narrative Elements	Use the "Magic Weave"
	    Categories
	        Character
	        Setting
	        Plot
	        Language
	            Personification, Alliteration, Diction, Metaphor, Simile, Irony, and so forth
	        Symbol
	        Tone
	        Mood

Quincunx	Quote
	    From the book of interest to the reader
	    On the outside of the finger holes
	Thinking
	    What you thought of the quote
	    On the inside corresponding to the quote
	Question
	    A question about the quote and thinking
	    On the inside flap of the thinking
	Answer
	    Answer to the question posed above
	    On the bottom of the opened flap

Figure 4.1 shows students working in their quincunxs. Notice how they have their books and re-enter the text to find their quotes and answers.

Fig. 4.1

Tie a strip of paper into a knot, crease and trace around it, open **Conflict Knots** the knot and you will find two arrows, write conflicts between the arrows. Collect all of the knots and open one from time to time for discussion.

Page 1 Title of book and authors name **Eight-Page Book**
Page 2 Quote from the book **or Quire**
Page 3 "This reminds me of ..."
Page 4 Quote from book
Page 5 "I think this means ..."
Page 6 Quote from book
Page 7 "This is important because ..."
    Could also be used with
            Interesting Fact, Detail, Main Idea, Summary,
            Picture I see in my mind ..., I still wonder ...

Fig. 4.2

Fig. 4.2

Character Trait Circle Web	Paper plate divided into 12 parts
	Fear
	Sorrow
	Apathy
	Joy
	Hate
	Pity
	Despair
	Wonder
	Pride
	Hope
	Anger
	Love
	Find examples of these in the novel.
Three-sided Pyramid	Outside triangles are used for drawing:
	Characters
	Settings
	Images
	Inside triangles are used to write:

Description
Quotes
Thoughts/Feelings

Fig. 4.3

Billboard or Character Review Diorama

* Write the name of the character.
* Give a physical description of the character using words that appeal to the five senses.
* Describe the characters behavior and actions. Describe the character doing some action.
* Describe or quote how the character acts and reacts around others.
* Describe the character through the eyes of another character in the book. Capture the attitude others have toward the character.
* List the four most prominent character traits the character exhibits.
* On the inside sides of the diorama write two examples of dialogue that typify the character, things that show what kind of person they are.

CASPAR Chart   Character
                    Adjectives
                    Setting
                    Problems
                    Action/Plot
                    Resolution

Literary Letter   Write a letter to a parent, relative, teacher, or a peer about
                            the book you are reading or some issue in the book you find
                            interesting or can relate to. Make connections between the book
                            and your personal experience. Rotate so that all students write
                            at least one letter to a parent, teacher, or peer.
                            Fig 4.4

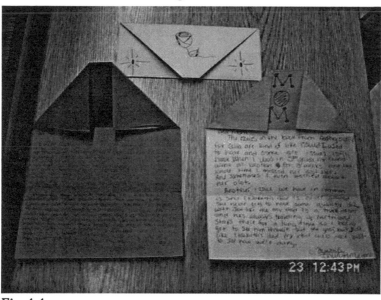

Fig. 4.4

Flip Book   Characterization
                 Plot
                 Sequencing
                 Cause/Effect

5 It's All *Downriver* From Here

A Novel Unit

Whatever we read together as a class is literature that I love and I think the students can relate to. When I stop being surprised or affected by a certain piece of literature, I stop teaching it. It must be fresh for me, so it can be fresh for the kids.

—Linda Rief

Once a novel is chosen and I have read through it at least once, I revisit it and decide where we want to stop reading. Depending on the novel, this could be after a chapter or two, or I may just assign reading up to certain page number in books that don't have chapters. I prefer not to divide the book up into equal parts to fit a six-week period or set amount of time. Instead, I create assignments for one section before reading on and finding a suitable breaking point for the next section. This way I do not end with the suspense hanging or in the middle of a plot twist. I find that when the story is good and the action intense, students read more, so the number of pages increases as the plot approaches the climax and resolution of the book. With some novels it's hard to stop students from finishing the book, even if I assign a break. I never discourage a student from reading to the end; however, I will caution them that if they read ahead, they may get confused with the assignments for a certain section and have to do some rereading to reacquaint themselves with the plot and characters' actions.

At the start of a new novel I do not assign too big a chunk of reading, just one large enough to get a feeling for what the book is about. I talk to the students about the different types of reading you have to do at the beginning of a novel, where the author is setting up the plot, characters, and settings, giving lots of description and information that has to be processed to understand what will happen later. I read part of the first chapter aloud to get the students started, and then turn it over to them to finish up. This gets students into the book and also helps them pronounce names, become familiar with vocabulary, and listen for the style of the author. During the read-aloud I will stop and point out specific ways the author crafts his or her writing and what to look for as they read.

As I reread the first section of the book, I look for what the author provides in terms of literary content as well as what is happening with the character, setting and plot. I distribute sticky notes (Tovani, 2004) as the students read silently in groups. For example:

> SSR (sustained silent reading).
>
> Read pages 79-119 in the novel *Breaking Rank*. I ask the students to record on sticky notes the conflicts they find in their reading.

To help students focus on the reading and have something ready for discussion the next week, sticky notes preserve what students have read and thought while they were reading. These notes also help students reenter the text and question what is going on. With each successive section of reading, I look for different devices and literary constructions for the students to capture on their sticky notes.

After I have reread a section I think about a topic students can connect to their lives and write about. The writing group (W) is all about trying to get students to connect the text to themselves. I usually focus on one of the characters in the section and their problems. Sometimes at the beginning of a novel, before the plot begins to take off, it is hard to do that, so I focus on what the characters' lives are like, putting students in their shoes. The other component of the Writing group is to reinforce writing skills learned through minilessons. Whatever the minilessons were for the novel, I expect to see evidence of their use in the students' writing.

As I think about a writing prompt for a section of reading, the literary devices and construction of that prompt, I usually end up creating thought-provoking questions and ideas for discussion. Some point usually stands out that the students need to know or focus on to understand the novel, so I use that to start the class novel discussion (CND). I say "start" because the discussion tends to move from its intended purpose to other topics that interest the students. Sometimes students delay discussion by asking clarification questions on the ideas they have written on their sticky notes. While the other groups work, I sit with the discussion group to both supervise and lend a hand in clarification. I do not participate other than to swing the topic back on track or ask questions, but I do listen and praise, helping the struggling readers understand good reading behavior. One of the questions I ask over and over is, "Where did you find that in the text?" This is my way of making them go back to find where they developed their opinions; this allows everyone in the group to see how information in a novel can be digested differently. I spend a lot of time during the first six weeks teaching the students how to discuss, constantly making them provide textual evidence for their answers, and using "Questioning the Author techniques" (Beck & McKeown, 1998).

For the independent work group (IND), I figure out what type of 3-D graphic organizer or other organizing tools best help students glean information out of that particular section of reading. Sometimes it is more a matter of emphasizing something that the author did and then having students decide the best way to convey that information. I find ways to make the information more challenging through the use of 3-D graphic organizers or some other tactic. I know students create flip charts more readily and complete them more eagerly than if I ask them to do the same task on a sheet of paper or on a worksheet.

The one group that is not necessarily tied to the novel is the journal group (J). This group works on bringing a piece of their own writing through to publication. More times than not this piece is connected to one of the novels that we have read in class, but it does not have to be. Students are writing at several different times in my class; they write in their response journals after SSR; they write in the writing group, the research group, and at times in the independent discussion group. They have a lot of writing to choose from and at times have a hard time deciding, which in itself contributes to higher level thinking. To help them, I have them share some of their writing with their classmates through the share strategies. On Fridays, instead of writing in their journals, they share in small groups, and I assign one of the share strategies so they get some feedback. This helps the students to see how others react to their writing and where they may possibly take their writing in the future.

Sharing also takes place in the first couple of weeks we are working on a novel. There is not yet enough information for new topics driven by the issues in the novel, so I ask students to share some of their writing and their thoughts about doing it. The topics of these early journals are usually about their family, memories generated through the use of Paula Brock's "Quick List," or topics that may have come up in the news. In the group, other students give feedback about what they saw or thought about as they wrote, as they listened, and as they heard what the plans for it were.

There are many opportunities for feedback on the students' writing as well as opportunities for the students to talk about writing. They learn from each other as much as they learn from me and from reading various authors. There is also opportunity for the students to try out the new things they hear from each other, read in books, or learn because of the minilessons I have taught, and usually their peers let them know whether their risk-takings were successful or sounded phony for their style. I do change the groups on a book-to-book basis so that students experience a variety of styles and different ways of thinking from the authors. I feel that sharing writing is as important a task in the choosing of a piece of writing for publication as is the process of writing itself.

I ask students to commit to one piece of writing after they have read through all they have written and shared their top choices. Many of the NJWPT/Abydos principles are in place as this goes through process. Most of the writing takes place outside of class while the assigned work in class is more revision and editing. As with anything, a break from it is necessary to refocus, and in this group students get a break from the novel and the novel gives them a break from their writing.

DOWNRIVER THROUGH THE NOVEL

To me, literacy is a word which describes a whole collection of behaviors, skills, knowledge, processes and attitudes. It has something to do with our ability to use language in our negotiations with the world. Often these negotiations are motivated by our desires to manipulate the world for our own benefit. Reading and Writing are two linguistic ways of conducting these negotiations. So are talking, listening, thinking, reflecting, and a host of other behaviors related to cognition and critical thinking.
—Brian Cambourne

I chose the YA novel *Downriver* by Will Hobbs to illustrate how I conduct reading/writing workshop because its action draws the reader through the novel as fast as the rivers are moving in the river rafting sections. I have found that struggling and reluctant readers like the fast pace, so they read the novel, especially once the other students start talking about it. I use this as one of the first novels in the year for that reason—to prove that the novels read in this class are exciting and worth their time. I also use this novel toward the beginning of the year because it exemplifies well written description and imagery, two areas sorely lacking in most students' writing. Besides, it helps students see how both are crafted and how they enhance a story. Frankly, I start early with these, so I won't have to read dry papers for the rest of the year!

Setting the students up for the action or plot of the novel, I simultaneously create background knowledge and foster anticipation. One group starts to read the novel, but the other four groups do not get to it until later in the week. Therefore, the initial assignments for these groups have nothing to do with the novel. Rather I give assignments that allow students to draw on their experiences and ultimately link them with main character, events, and issues in *Downriver*. Their assignment sheet (Fig. 5.1) actually runs a week behind the reading to ensure that all students have had the opportunity to read the given section before using the information in an assignment.

Fig. 5.1

See page six for an explanation of groups and schedule.

**ASSIGNMENTS
WEEK ONE
FOR
DOWNRIVER**

Read pages one to twenty-four in *Downriver* by Will Hobbs. Use sticky notes to mark thoughts or imagery that "stick out" in your mind as you read.

**SSR
Group Work**

Write about a time you got into trouble and were severely punished.
    Include: How did you feel at the time about the person who punished you? How did you feel after a period of time had passed and it was all behind you? How did it affect the relationship between the two of you?

**W
Group Work**

Discuss books the people in your group have read that were adventure stories. Talk about how these books are typically written. What do you expect from an adventure book? Also talk about what types of characters and settings you find. Someone in the group takes notes and hands them in at the end of the period.

**CND
Group Work**

IND
Group Work

Write about a time you have been camping, fishing or done something in, around, or by a river. Include how you felt and what the water made you think about. Try to include a descriptive section of your favorite spot by the river. Use all of your senses in your description.

J
Group Work

Look over your journal entries and pick a piece to take through the process. Think about our minilessons about writing. Try to add something that you've learned to your writing. Play with a piece of writing; try something totally different: add dialogue, description, metaphor, depth of thought, or another scene, anything to change the way the piece reads.

Teacher Tasks
for Week One
Downriver

I teach minilessons on the use of the senses in description (sensory imagery) and the "Sensuous Metaphor" (Carroll & Wilson, 162-168). Doing this first helps students visualize as they read *Downriver*. I space the minilessons out with a day or two in between to see how the students incorporate them into their writings. It is more worthwhile to immediately see how the students use what I taught them so I am able to help them individually if they are struggling. Because students are in each group for only one day, it takes a couple of days for some of them to get a chance to use a new strategy, so I don't like to pile too much on them at one time.

Specifics for
SSR
Group

Students read the first section of the novel. Because I want them to pay particular attention to action (plot) and setting, I ask them to write sticky notes on the imagery they notice. By taking notes as they read, they work the information into their brains more than one time; and, as research has shown, that enhances long-term memory. Writing sticky notes does not interrupt their reading, because they only stop when something strikes them or sticks out in the reading. This is also good training because good readers stop and make mental notes all the time as they read. The sticky notes also give students something concrete to reference when they discuss each section in their discussion group (CND).

Specifics for
W
Group

Since the novel starts begins with the main character at a camp for troubled teens, I establish background experience for the students through an assignment about troubles they have been in and the consequences they suffered. Writing about themselves while dealing with a subject that is similar to the plight of the main character, helps students relate to the main character and quickly get into the book. It doesn't seem to matter if the main character is a girl or a boy; students empathize better when they relate to things they have experienced. So, in the writing prompt I include questions or criteria to guide the students' thinking. I remind them of the minilessons and encourage them to consider them as further possibilities for their writing. I do not expect their first attempts to be awe inspiring, but I do expect to see evidence that they tried. As the year moves along and they have had more practice, I raise my expectations and expect them to inspire me.

Through discussion, I foster knowledge of the genre we are reading. I include topics related to the students' independent reading to show how everything connects and how important all reading is but in different ways. As I monitor other groups, making sure they understand what they should be doing, students share the books they have read and talk about them. By the time they finish, I have returned, so we start to discuss the genre and the things we have found or think we will find that all these books in this genre have in common. In addition to showing the worth of reading, the book share also has the benefit of getting the students excited about different books. Allowing them to hear a little bit about them offers options. The next time they have to choose a book, they have several from which to choose. In all discussions, the group has a recorder and eventually each member of the group is recorder at least once. They record the nuts and bolts of the discussion so students may go back to those records later if they want to include it in their writing something discussed or if they want to bring out a talking point again at a later date. If I do not have time to join the discussion, I collect the notes to look them over and evaluate what the students discussed.

Specifics for SND Group

Usually I have a brief activity or 3-D graphic organizer for the students to work on, but because this is the beginning of the novel, I foster connections to their experience and a relationship with the characters and setting of the book. Since the students have already written from the perspective of themselves about a character-like problem, this time they write to evoke memories about the setting of the story. Having the students write about a setting they remember dealing with water using sensory imagery brings out the sound and feel of water, something that enhances the descriptions in the novel, something plot intensive. This assignment also utilizes the minilesson taught during the week.

Specifics for IND Group

This group explores their own writing and attempts to do something new with it. They have many entries in their journal by this time from the journal writing they have done during the first part of the block class. During workshop, I ask them to commit to one of these pieces to take through to publication; therefore, during this first week I expect them to take some time to reread their writings, choosing one or two they want to write more about, and trying some new writing strategies or techniques. Once again this group will be expected to apply some of the minilessons to their writing. They practice and explore how these techniques fit into

Specifics for J Group

ASSIGNMENTS
WEEK TWO
FOR
DOWNRIVER

their style and voice. They also work on craft.

SSR
Group Work

Read pages 25-53 in *Downriver* by Will Hobbs. Use sticky notes to jot down thoughts about the different characters.

W
Group Work

Write about a situation when you counted on someone for help and did not get it, so you had to turn to someone else. Include details of what the person was supposed to help you with, why they didn't help or how they failed to help, and how you felt about it.

CND
Group Work

Discuss what you know about the characters of the novel so far. Who are they? What are they like? Why they are there? What are the group dynamics and interactions? What language is used to help you know these things? Have someone record your discussion and turn it in.

IND
Group Work

Draw a picture of one of your biggest fears. Make the drawing as scary as it is in your mind while at the same time showing others what your fear is. Be sure to use color to intensify the images you draw.

J
Group Work

Write about the big fear in your life. Include why, what led to it, how it incapacitates you, and what you might try to get over it.

TEACHER TASKS
FOR WEEK TWO
DOWNRIVER

This week's minilessons are on imagery, the use of color, and characterization. These minilessons extend the descriptive writing of last week, but concentrate more on the effect descriptive writing has on the audience—the reader. I point out how authors emphasize specific scenes through the use of color—how color sets the mood and tone of a book. I also introduce characterization and how authors bring characters to life, what strategies they use to get readers to know and understand a character, and why some characters seem more alive than others.

Although I shift the focus to reading and comprehension, writing continues to be incorporated. Any time we talk about reading and the understanding of reading, we tie what we have read back to what the author did and how the author crafted the work to evoke feeling and thinking. In other words, students apply the author's strategies to their own writing to elicit the same results.

Specifics for
SSR
Group

I design the reading assignment so students get through a section in one period. After the first two sections in the novel, I make some reading assignments shorter than others because there is so much information students have to know before they understand and move along with the plot. Novels differ but I have found that usually after two sections of reading or about four chapters, students have enough information to read more quickly. We talk about reading paces on and off throughout the year when we read silently together, sharing parts of different books as examples. The sticky notes for this week focus on the minilessons of imagery, color, and characterization. By this time Hobbs has given enough information on most of the characters for students to make some generalizations about them. Students pick out things about the characters they can talk about, and we compare how different readers key into different aspects of characters, making meaningful generalizations based on the textual evidence and students' experiences.

Writing this week deals with developing empathy of common experiences with the characters in the novel. Previously, in the first section of *Downriver*, the main character feels like her father let her down. I want students to think of a time when someone disappointed them. I hope to show students that even though their disappointment may not have been on the same scale as the main character's, they still probably share some of the same feelings. Once again I include criteria for the students to add into their compositions, and I expect them to incorporate information from the past minilessons.

Specifics for W Group

During discussion, students focus on the introduction of the characters in *Downriver*. How did the author achieve that introduction? What are the exact words (diction) we first read about a character important? I bring out the importance of first impressions not only in a novel but also in life. I stress the importance of word choice in developing a character. This discussion usually allows students to reference their sticky notes from this week, but I keep discussion centered on the first section of reading, leaving the sticky note information for an assignment and for their individual interpretations at a later time.

Specifics for CND Group

Drawing helps the reading skill of visualization. I encourage drawing a couple of times during the reading of a novel to help the students work on this skill. In this case, drawing also ties the minilessons on imagery and color to the main character. In the novel the main character faces some of her fears at the wilderness camp, so this assignment helps students come closer to and walk in the character's shoes. Some students understand more about how the character feels through this assignment than if I ask them to write about it. Through drawing, some visual learners connect and make meaning. I vary the activities to reach all of the learning styles of my students. Even when I read the same novel from year after year, I change some of the assignments and activities depending on how the

Specifics for IND Group

students best learn.

Specifics for J Group   This journal group assignment gives students something personal to write about in order to get their feelings on paper. As I tell the students, "I will not read this entry if you do not want me to." I think some novels act as therapy, give us clues or glimpses into how people handle problems differently, and we can take those ideas and apply them to our own lives. Just because the book is fiction doesn't mean that the premises or actions of the character are not based on real life. I ask the students to write about their lives in parallel situations. They examine their past to see if there is a story waiting to be written. We talk about how authors call upon their own experiences to create stories. So from time to time, I ask students to write about themselves and to dig deep into their emotions and feelings.

ASSIGNMENTS WEEK THREE FOR DOWNRIVER

SSR Group Work   Read pages 54-83 in *Downriver* by Will Hobbs. Use sticky notes to jot down what you think is important in this section of reading.

W Group Work   Write about a time when your home seemed far away and you really missed its comforts. Include sensory imagery to help your audience understand why you missed being there.

CND Group Work   Discuss what you think will happen from this point on in *Downriver*. Make specific predictions about the characters based on what you know about them so far. Where will this all end? Write your predictions, be ready to hand in and/or post on the wall.

IND Group Work   Create a flipbook out of five sheets of paper. Divide it into ten sections, one for each of the nine characters and the final one for a generalization. Write a description of each character; include specific sensory imagery from the novel as textual evidence. Also include their attitudes and their backgrounds.

J Group Work   Look back through your journal and reread what you have written about yourself. Choose one to continue writing through to publication but add more to it. Make a commitment to this writing that you will be use it for the next couple of weeks.

The minilessons this week include drawing conclusions, outcomes, and punctuation, especially the four most common uses of the comma. Since the plot of the novel is pretty well underway, my minilesson on drawing conclusions is based on the information we have already read. We discuss: What types of things can we figure out based on what the author tells us and our experience or background? It is important to help students realize that we all regard the same piece of text differently depending on our experience and background. To help students understand there is no right or wrong answer to many questions dealing with interpreting a novel, I stress informed answers, ones backed by textual evidence.

The minilesson about outcomes follows along the same lines as drawing conclusions because the two are closely related. I teach them back-to-back so students realize the differences and similarities in the two, showing them that outcomes are a more global or larger look at the information read.

After teaching imagery and description, students' writing either gets choppy with short sentences or their sentences lengthen and end up becoming run-on sentences. This is a perfect time to teach the four most often used rules for commas, the same lesson taught during the NJWPT/Abydos summer institute. After the minilesson I challenge students to reenter their writing and revise their sentences using the comma rules. I caution them they may also find details that need to be added or deleted in the process—after all writing is recursive.

With *Downriver's* plot in full swing, students focus on what they think is important information. Struggling students often have problems discerning what is important in the plot from just extra information. They get confused easily with all of the information they read and think everything is vital to understanding the book. If I ask students to take notes on what they feel is important, then compare their notes with those other students have written—they learn faster from each other in small groups than they do from me. The section they are reading this week is about what happens when the teenagers take off on their own, something that is of high interest to this grade level. This theme also makes for interesting notes on what students feel is important.

The writing assignment for this section invites students to convey a feeling and the reason behind that feeling to a specific audience. We have talked about description and imagery and have studied examples of what authors do, so I want to see what students accomplish in their writing and how they put it all together. In this process they are once again identifying with the main character in *Downriver* and the way she feels.

Teacher Tasks for Week Three Downriver

Specifics for SSR Group

Specifics for W Group

Keeping the students' interested in a novel is part of the effort to get them to read. With this novel, it is not hard to sustain their interest because Hobbs has done a wonderful job of keeping the book flowing with action after action, just like the wild ride down a whitewater river. I have found in novels with slower action or those taking longer for plot development, identification with the main character and what or how the students would handle the same situations also occurs more slowly. But patience and a variety of strategies pay off because they foster analytical thinking, making that skill part of how students begin to think when they read independently.

Specifics for CND Group   I sit in on the discussions this week to help the students use the strategies we talked about in the minilessons on drawing conclusions and outcomes. Another task they must complete is a chart of their predictions with each prediction followed by textual evidence as support. These charts are posted on the wall so other groups and other classes can read them and compare. There is no better teaching or learning tool than comparing one's work to that of others to see if anything was missed. A saying I once heard fits, "There is no one person as smart as all of us." Individually we can accomplish much but collectively we can accomplish more.

Specifics for IND Group   This assignment is all about students using the sticky notes they took about the characters while reading last week. They use a 3-D organizer, the flipbook, to organize the information on all nine characters. They take notes in their flipbooks to capture impressions as they continue to read the novel. It is important for students to identify attitudes and the way a character reacts or interacts with other characters, which is another facet of understanding plot and prediction. Most of the assignments in the independent work group are designed to help students learn the habits of a good reader. Fig. 5.2 shows an example of the flip book.

Specifics for J Group   Again the students review and reread their own writing, which helps them see the progress they have made and also revisits some of the ideas they started but have forgotten. They choose a piece of writing and stick with until it reaches the published stage. Most students choose the piece they started to work on two weeks ago, but others who already narrowed their choices, now have to make the choice of what to continue writing. If they ask me which they should choose, I stay neutral and out of the decision. I advise the class when I talk about this assignment that they want to choose a piece of writing where there is still more to write, one they remember as vividly as possible. The piece should interest them so much they don't mind working on it for the next couple of weeks. There are always a few students who still do not know what they will be working on by the end of the period, but they know they must have it ready for next week. Fig. 5.3 shows students working in their journals.

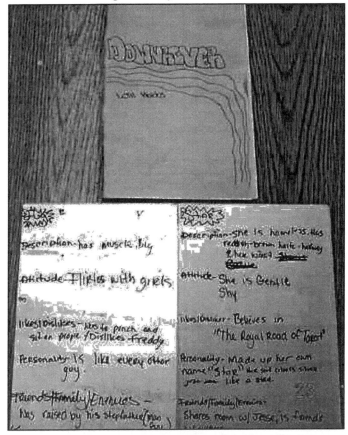

Fig 5.2

Fig 5.3

SSR
Group Work

Read pages 84-121 in *Downriver* by Will Hobbs. Use sticky notes to infer what you think might happen as the story continues and comment on those things that did happen as you predicted.

W
Group Work

Write about something you did that was both thrilling and scary at the same time, something that gave you a feeling of satisfaction and when you were finished made you feel like you had accomplished something.

CND
Group Work

Discuss the descriptions of the whitewater adventures in this section of the novel. Talk about how Hobbs uses words and syntax to accomplish the up-and-down, side-to-side motions as well as the speed of the ride. Write these words and descriptors down with your explanations.

IND
Group Work

Create a diorama pop-up with a drawing of one of the whitewater scenes as you picture it. Below the scene write the description from the book. On the sides of the pop-up draw the walls of the canyon. Think back to movies or pictures you have seen about river rafting to help you with your imagination and drawing.

J
Group Work

Using the journal entry that you chose in week three, continue to write, making sure to add description and imagery where they are needed. Be prepared to have a rough draft completed next week.

TEACHER
TASKS FOR
WEEK FOUR
DOWNRIVER

In week four I teach only one minilesson on word choice and usage. Authors choose their words carefully, especially when they describe characters, settings, or parts of the plot. I want students to think about how the words they write affect the piece they are writing and how the words they read affect their depth of comprehension of the novel. Once again students see how closely reading and writing link, how one affects the other, and how one strategy affects both disciplines. This minilesson includes the use of a thesaurus and the multiple meanings of words. The remainder of the week I conduct reading/writing conferences with the students, talking to them about the piece they decided to write about and how they are doing with their independent reading, as well as any problems they are having with the class novel. I do this at least twice during the six-week period, the first time when I meet with everyone; the second time when I meet with only those who wish to meet with me.

Following the discussion from last week, students write sticky notes about their predictions and make new predictions based on new information they uncover as they read. Their reading is getting to the point of the climax, so students read rapidly because of the rising action. I assign a few more pages, but I am careful of the breaking point, interrupting a plot, or cutting the students off in a place where they are left hanging. I have found that when I did do that the students either read ahead anyway to find out what happened or they gave up on the story because I ruined the flow of the book for them and they lost interest. With some novels I let the students finish the book early because the plot travels so fast and furious there really is no breaking point. It is a delicate balance to find a breaking point and still keep the students involved.

Specifics for SSR Group

Helping students get in touch with their emotions is both therapeutic and uncovers good subjects for writing. People are more apt to vividly remember things attached to strong emotions; students are no different and, therefore, are better able to describe them when they write. Novels are about helping students learn about who they are and what they would or would not do if put in the same situation as the characters in the novel. Therefore I choose the novels I read with the class with that in mind, looking for issues that the students deal with in their lives. Writing about those issues is one way to raise awareness and teach lessons.

Specifics for W Group

The discussion this week follows on the heels of the minilesson and is actually guided practice meant to make the lesson more concrete. Hobbs does a great job of making the reader feel the motion and speed of the river, and guiding students to discover how he does that helps them analyze the novel for themselves. Later, it helps them discover how they can do the same thing as they write. Thus Hobbs creates both a good read and a mentor text for students. Students become readers who write and writers who read. They discover they had never thought about certain things as a reader, but as a writer they think about craft in order to get *their* readers engaged and hold their interest. This provides the perfect talking point about varying sentence length and the effects it has on the pace of reading, suspense, and plot development. Often that becomes a micro-minilesson.

Specifics for CND Group

The pop-up diorama (Fig. 5.4) combines a 3-D graphic organizer with student choices from the text. This form of response addresses students' various learning styles and connects art, imagery, and engagement with the text; it also gives students ownership through choice. Many students have never heard of visualizing; they dislike reading long stories because they complain there is too much information. They tell me, "Sir, I get

Specifics for IND Group

lost in all of those words." When I model making movies in my head, they look at me like I am crazy. Yet all year long as we read, I talk to them about the importance of creating pictures in their heads, about not worrying about getting it exactly but approximating it. Then I model connecting that approximation with something they already know and letting their imagination conform it to the story.

The diorama exemplifies how I get students started on that track. Most of them have not been whitewater rafting nor have ever seen a raft, so they rely on what the novel tells them coupled with possibly something on TV or in the movies. It is interesting to see how differently the other students interpret the same scenes. Again they learn from what others think and write.

Pop-up Diorama

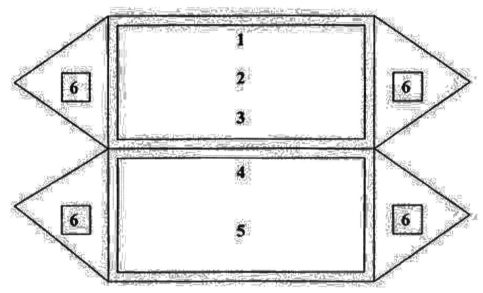

Fig 5.4

Directions for Written Responses in Pop-up Diorama

1. Write the name of the character.
2. Give a physical description of the character using words that appeal to the five senses.
3. Describe the characters behavior and actions. Describe the character doing some action.
4. Describe or quote how the character acts and reacts around others.
5. Describe the character through the eyes of another character in the book. Capture the attitude others have toward the character.
6. List the four most prominent character traits the character exhibits.

On the inside sides of the diorama write two examples of dialogue that typify the character, things that show what kind of person he or she is.

To create the Diorama:

1. Fold a sheet of 8.5 X11 paper in half "hotdog" style.
2. Unfold. Then fold it in half the other way.
3. Unfold. Placing the paper in front of you 'hotdog' style. Fold the edges in to the middle. (left and right sides)
4. Keeping it folded. Pick up one flap and cut along the midpoint line to the edge.
5. Do the same with the other flap.
6. Now take the upper corner of one flap and fold it back diagonally so that the point is on the outside edge and the side matches up with that edge.
7. Do the same to the other three corners of the flaps.
8. Keeping the flaps closed fold the entire thing in half along the cuts.
9. When you open it back up 90%, slip the sides over one another so that they interlock.

This week the journal group works on the paper they have chosen to take through the writing process. I make sure they include all the things we have covered from the novel and Hobbs' craft. They continue writing outside of the classroom, using the class time mainly to consult tools such as dictionaries and thesauri, the Internet, or other sources they need to make progress. I am available for conferences, usually at the end of the period on any given day. This week I get a chance to talk to each of them about their progress and plans for their paper. I do not lead the conference but encourage them to ask questions about what they need; I want to know where they are headed with the paper and how they intend to get there.

Read pages 122-166 in *Downriver* by Will Hobbs. Use sticky notes to record your observations as you read and as the information starts to make sense or leads you to some conclusion.

W
Group Work
Write about a setting you remember because of its beauty. Try to recreate that beauty with words and through imagery. Use color like you would in a drawing but add another dimension by tying it to one of the five senses.

CND
Group Work
Discuss the characters in the novel again. Use your flipbooks on the characters and add new information that you discover through your group. Focus on group dynamics, who interacts with whom and why? The flipbooks are due at the end of the period.

IND
Group Work
Using the "Wheel of Emotions," find two examples of each emotion in the novel and write them on another sheet of paper. Try to involve as many characters as possible.

J
Group Work
Using the Summarizing Share Strategy, read your piece to a small group and listen to the feedback to see if what they heard what you intended. Listeners respond by writing what they think is your main idea. Then they summarize their main idea in one word, and then with a synonym. Each person in the group will read and respond. (Fig. 5.5)

Fig 5.5

This week we talk about depth in writing. How do authors make us think and feel about what is going on in the story? The minilessons will be "depth charging" (Carroll) and "thought shots" (Lane), strategies to get students adding that extra something to their writing. I start with depth charging to accustom students to vertical elaboration. They add more after a sentence they have already written to achieve insight and produce depth. I then teach "thought shots." Because they already have a foundation for adding information with depth charging, they just have to shift their thinking a little from characterization to thinking processes. These two strategies make a huge difference in the quality of students' writing. I reteach these minilessons a couple of more times throughout the year to make sure the students internalize them and add them naturally into their writing. By the end of the year, depth is not something they have to add to their writing but something they authentically imbed in their writing.

Teacher Tasks for Week Five Downriver

The action is really moving in the novel at this point—as they say, "the plot thickens," so I don't interrupt the reading too much and take the fun out of it. I do, however, want students to think about what they are reading. So I slow them a little by having them read to find *new* information about the plots that are underway, taking notes when they draw a conclusion or come across something they think may be important later on in the novel. I want my students to be constantly thinking while they read and the sticky notes are a concrete way to accomplish this. As the year progresses I use sticky notes less and less as students internalize the process. In order to train the brain to do something, it has to be thought about and worked through—then gradually it becomes a subconscious process.

Specifics for SSR Group

Writing this week is about setting instead of characters. I emphasize the setting because it parallels Hobbs's descriptions of the scenery and side canyons, and it helps to make the book more realistic. I want students to notice setting and take time to be creative, practicing writing what they picture in their minds. I model creating descriptions as real as the pictures I see in my head. I tap again the minilessons taught earlier in the novel.

Specifics for W Group

Discussion this week focuses on the group dynamics and the interactions of the characters. Students have been working on adding information to their flipbooks for two weeks as they read and discuss. During this discussion they see how what they found differs from others in their group. Students tackle not only how people act in *Downriver* but also how they, as readers, feel towards the characters. This discussion usually becomes pretty lively as differences of opinion about how

Specifics for CND Group

characters are expressed. Many differences of opinion occur because of the experiences of the students. I monitor the discussion—ever ready to nudge students to reenter the novel for the information that led them to their assumptions and opinions. This discussion exemplifies how experience changes our views and understanding of what we read.

Specifics for IND Group   The "Wheel of Emotions," (Fig. 5.6) a 3-D graphic organizer I learned during the TAKS Relief™ Week presented by Carroll and Wilson, shows students the range of emotions that happen in a novel. Many times when students write a story, they limit their telling to one or two emotions. By having them give two examples for each emotion on the wheel, they quickly see there is more they can do through their writing. It also gives them many more ideas about how to craft those emotions.

The first task using the "Wheel of Emotion" is to have the students define each emotion so they know what to look for in the novel. After this, they skim and scan the novel for examples of each emotion. The examples do not have to necessarily come from the same character, but students usually find the main character is a rich lode to tap. Paralleling this assignment, I talk about character traits as closely related to the emotions. This tie-in helps students grasp the meaning of a trait.

Specifics for J Group   Since there is about a week left in the six-week period, I want students to get a feel for what others think about their writing. Regardless of whether they have or have not completed their paper, each student reads it to their group. We use the same process we used in the NJWPT/Abydos summer institute: the reader reads his/her paper through twice: listeners listen and focus on the main idea or central tenant; they synopsize the main idea in one word. Each sharing is different because each listener has a different response. Through this strategy, authors check if what they intended for the audience was what the audience got. When the listeners respond with a main idea and explain their answer, they tell the author what they understood the paper to be about and why; it is the *why* that is important to the author. If the audience's interpretation differs from the author's intention, the author notes that. If the author chooses to fix the problem by deeper revision, it is his/her choice. Ultimately it is up to the author to be happy with the paper, so revision at this point is up to the author.

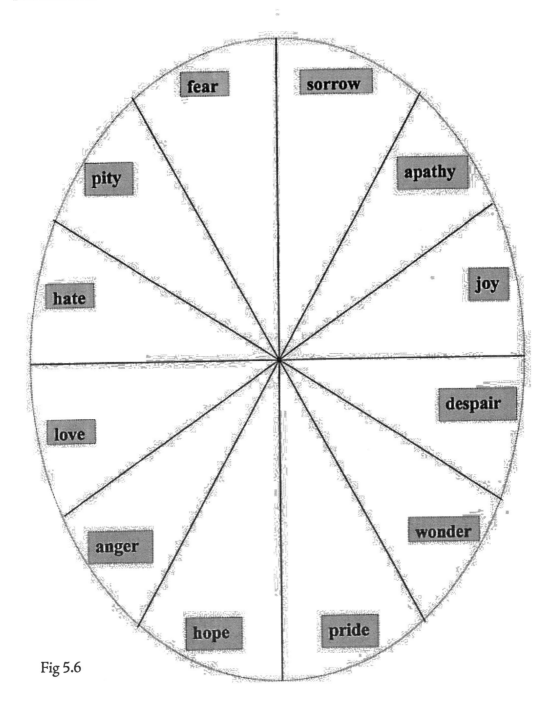

Fig 5.6

SSR
Group Work
Begin on 167 and read to the conclusion of *Downriver*. Use sticky notes to record information about how the accuracy of your predictions.

W
Group Work
Write about what it is like to persuade a group of people to do something that differs from what the leader would like to do. Give real-life examples of this dilemma and describe what happened. Also write suggestions or ideas to persuade a group to take a different path or make a different decision.

CND
Group Work
Discuss the word *betrayal* and its meaning in the context of the novel. Reenter the novel to find instances of betrayal and how those betrayed overcame the situation. Take notes and be prepared to turn them in at the end of the period.

IND
Group Work
Reenter the novel to find incidents in the plot of the highest intensity. Choose five and chart them on a graph. Record the intensity and excitement as if they were readouts from a heart monitor. Make sure to include a good summary of each incident so that others will know what plot line or event you are recording.

J
Group Work
Using the feedback from your share session, make final adjustments to your paper and then ratiocinate using the four codes: "to be" verbs, repeated words, sentence length, and sentence beginnings. When looking at sentence length, check for comma usage. A final rough draft is due next week.

Teacher Tasks
for Week Six
Downriver
     As we draw to the end of *Downriver*, I want the students organize their information, so I present a minilesson on making generalizations. They have enough information from *Downriver* and their independent novel to make some generalizations. I use *Downriver* as the model and then have the students make some generalizations from their independent reading. Then we share and compare and even make generalization about making generalizations! At the end of the week, we take time to "clock" on the paper they are writing in the journal group (J). On that Friday, I change the schedule; we do workshop first, which gives all students a chance to finish their papers and an opportunity to get positive feedback through clocking. If there is any time left, we finish the class by reading.

As students finish reading, I want them to think about what they learned from the novel, so I ask them to write sticky notes about their predictions and outcomes. This helps tie into the minilessons on drawing conclusions and outcomes from earlier in the novel. Students usually have mixed feelings about the ending, so I encourage them to talk about what they thought within their group. This really depends on how fast they've read and how far ahead they've gotten in the last two weeks. I allow the students to read ahead once the climax has been reached to discover what the resolution will be. In *Downriver*, Hobbs does an excellent job of keeping the reader hooked until the end by extending the action. Many students can't wait to finish the book, so I add the discussion component when I give the directions for the groups.

Specifics for SSR Group

The writing group works on a persuasive paper this week, persuading a group from doing something already in motion. This assignment intends to make students think ahead about their futures and what to do if they find themselves in a similar situation. The group dynamics and mob rule mentalities that come up in this novel are similar to events that happened in my life around that age--not whitewater rafting—but small groups clashing with clashes within groups. Had I had a chance to think about these situations before they occurred or had I read information about how someone else handled these problems, I would have done a better job myself. I always think of something I should have done better after it happened, so this is my way of giving students a chance to think of something before it happens so they have a model.

Specifics for W Group

Discussion begins with *betrayal* as one of the themes in the novel. After the students talk about the major betrayals in the book, we move to those that were not as obvious, e.g. a group member disappearing before the raft trip got started or the betrayals within the characters themselves. The discussion expands to other themes the students have found supported by their examples and evidence. Students chart this information to be posted on the walls.

Specifics for CND Group

This assignment is an adaptation of the telling share strategy. During the telling share, listeners chart the writing with lines like an EKG readout. In this assignment students pick the top five events from the story, put them in their proper sequence, and then chart them like an EKG. I am interested how different students chose different events and how others rate these same events. This is also an excellent way to help students review what happened in the novel before writing their final paper.

Specifics for IND Group

Specifics for J Group

Students ratiocinate their papers during this last week. They use the first four techniques because they are the most beneficial in helping students see what their paper looks and sounds like before the final revision. Eliminating the "be" verbs adds strength and power to the writing, deleting repeated words adds clarity, checking the sentence length adds depth, and noting sentence beginnings adds variety. All four techniques make the paper more focused, organized, and enjoyable. After the papers have been ratiocinated, the students fix what they want to fix, then at the end of the week we "clock" to take care of mechanics and grammar. In the week that follows, students polish what was wrong and turn in their pieces, which I usually publish in the hallway.

Assignment Week Seven For Downriver

Create a CASPER chart (Fig. 5.7) for the novel *Downriver* by Will Hobbs. This will take four sheets of paper to allow enough room for all the characters in the novel. Make sure to spend time considering appropriate adjectives that apply to each character and consider their motivations and actions throughout the novel.

The acronym for the typical CASPAR chart stands for Character, Adjective, Setting, Problem, Action/Plot, and Resolution. The only thing that changes for this version is the second "A" –Action/Plot; instead there is an "E" for **Ethics**. In the Ethics section, examine how the characters behave towards the others in the group and characterize what type of person they are. Present thoughts and opinions about the characters as well as feelings about how they conduct themselves.

In the setting section, list the memorable images in of the novel.

For each problem there should be a corresponding answer in the Resolution category.

Answer each section in detail. If there is not enough space, write on the back of the chart. Utilize space wisely while writing but write legibly. (Fig. 5.8)

The Final

The CASPER chart is an optional assignment used to wrap up the novel. I do not believe that tests are an accurate way to access a students' understanding of something they've read. As I have said, students need to understand there are many ways to look at information presented in a novel; as long as they base their understanding or opinions on the text and their experiences, they are not wrong. A test does not offer that leeway, but a writing assignment or 3-D graphic organizer such as the CASPER chart does. I find it does a great job of allowing me to assess whether students comprehend the novel while still permitting individual expression. I added the section on ethics because of the beautiful way it was brought forward in *Downriver*. I realized that the ethics in a situation is an important issue for teenagers, one they need to learn to deal with.

C	A	S	P	E	R

Fig 5.7

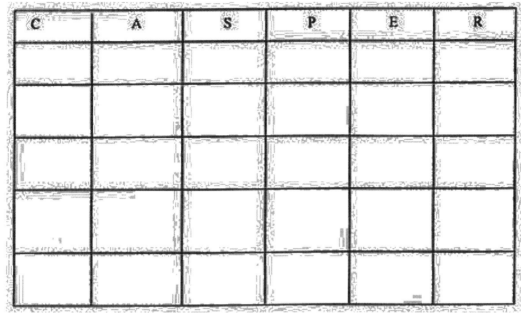

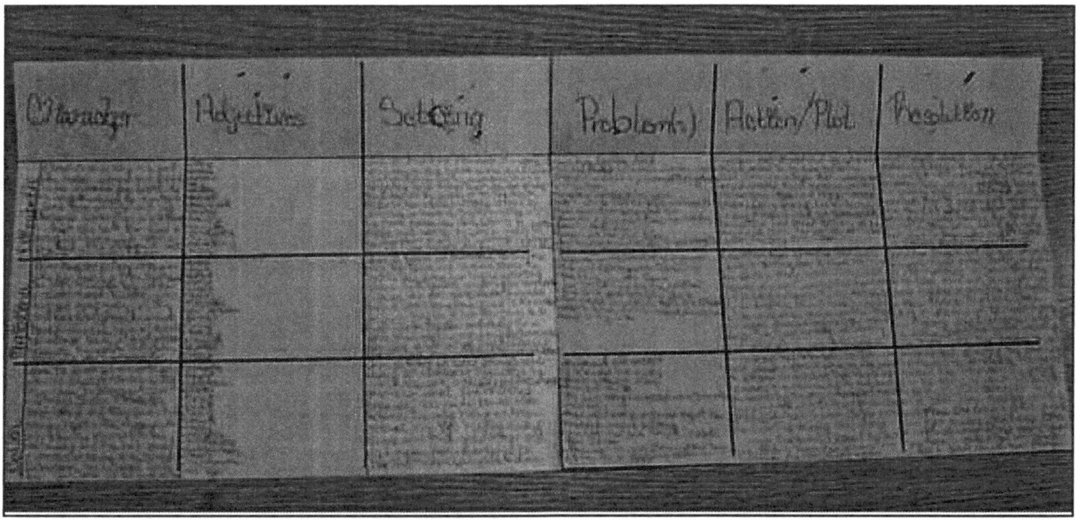

Fig 5.8

6 : Environment

Just as I settled back to my book, The Education of Little Tree (1987) by Forest Carter, on this October Friday morning, a teacher cranes his hand around the frame of the door. He steps over sprawled bodies, bends down, and whispers to me, "Boy, you sure planned hard for this lesson."

I am somewhat annoyed by this interruption, but take the time to glance around the room. There is hardly a sound. Marissa turns a page of The Great Gilly Hopkins (Paterson, 1978). Missy's face is intent, almost worried, as she reads Go ask Alice (Anonymous, 1978). Julie cradles Taking Terri Mueller (Mazer, 1983) in her lap. George is halfway through Never Cry Wolf (Mowat, 1981).

Mandy and Jen are conferencing quietly about a piece of writing about Mandy's grandmother. Val is revising a mystery piece she "just got an idea for." Brandon, who just read It Was a Dark and Stormy Night (Rice, 1987), is writing out some of his own best "worst" leads for the Bulwer-Lytton "bad" writing contest.

There is a commotion in the hallway as students pass. Across from us, the class is very loud while they wait for the teacher. Pat, one of my eighth graders, stands and walks slowly to the door, stepping over classmates, eyes remaining fixed on One Child (Hayden, 1980). He reaches out, feels for the knob, and pulls the door shut, never missing a word as he and Sheila, the main character, sink back down into his chair.

My colleague is right. I have prepared very hard for this lesson.
—Linda Rief, *Seeking Diversity*, 20.

When I read what Rief had written, I knew exactly what she was talking about. I get the same comments from my colleagues, in addition to some comment about the kids probably falling asleep because of the lack of lighting. I am often told (second or third hand) that others who venture by my open door or look in the window wonder when I teach because all my students ever do is read and write. I have had administrators conference with me after a walk through and tell me there needs to be more rigor. I invite them to spend a little more time in the room, do what the students are doing, and see if that doesn't change their minds. In every case they have not bothered me again; in fact, they often send other teachers to my room to observe. As Linda Rief points out in her vignette, it is not easy to achieve but when we do, it is well worth it.

Think about where you most like to read; is it in a stiff chair at a table or desk? When I first started Sustained Silent Reading (SSR) in my classroom, I was constantly fidgeting and wishing for a more comfortable place to sit. At that time we were remodeling our house and no longer wanted the couch and love seat we had had for years. I decided both would be ideal for the classroom, so I took them to school to create a reading nook. I found some carpet remnants and soon had a mini living room in the corner of my class. The students absolutely loved it, and I found that those who were reluctant or fidgety readers at their desk actually settled in to read for the long haul on the couch or floor. Of course there had to be some new rules negotiated and times established for the use of the couches and reading area, but it did not take us long to come up with them. (Fig. 6.1)

Fig 6.1

As the year progressed students suggested throw pillows and soft things to cushion those who liked to sit in a corner or on the floor. I also brought in a couple of end tables and a coffee table I found at a garage sale. As teachers visited my room, they offered other furniture they no longer used, so I added a recliner and a pappasan chair. Soon the room was filled with so much comfortable furniture, I had to limit what else I could bring in. What we all liked best were the throw pillows; they didn't take up much space, were easily stacked in a corner, and made everything about reading easier.

I continued this for a few years—going through one couch and the recliner. I kept finding replacements as the years passed until I had fewer pieces of school furniture and more pieces of the comfortable furniture in my room. The students adapt and like to sit on the couches during lessons; some even prefer the floor surrounded by pillows. As long as they are paying attention and working I don't mind where they sit. There is always the adjustment period at the beginning of the year because students have never had a classroom so comfortable, one that looks like a living area in their house. But after the rules are defined and tested, they settle in, are more calm and relaxed, and more predisposed to learn and produce. (Fig. 6.2)

Fig 6.2

I will never get rid of all of the tables and chairs in my room because I know from experience that there are some students that need or enjoy that type of environment for working. I, for one, am more comfortable writing at a table than on the couch with the tablet on my lap or a pillow, but limber, young students all like something a little different, so I try to provide a variety of options. Each year I ask students where they like to read and work and what suggestions they have for my room. I use the suggestions that sound good, are easy to provide, and will not be a distraction to learning.

Another unique facet in my room is the lighting. When students first walk into my room they immediately notice the dimmer lighting. It is more subdued than any other classroom. I do not turn on the fluorescent lighting in the ceiling; instead I use indirect lighting from six floor lamps and two table lamps. Research has shown that fluorescent lighting with its high speed flickering can agitate students, especially those with Attention Deficit Disorders. I was skeptical of this research at first but decided to try indirect lighting on a trial basis. I bought some cheap floor lamps on clearance and put them in the corners of the room and turned off the ceiling lights. When the students questioned this, I just told them I was tired of the bright lights and wanted to see if this would work. I kept them off for two days and then turned them back on. When I did I was surprised because the students complained and wanted them off again. I asked them about the adequacy of light for reading, and they suggested a couple of more lights were needed toward the middle of the room, which I bought, and from then on indirect lighting has been a surprising success.

I noticed those students who fidgeted and squirmed were calmer, those who often got out of their seats to sharpen pencils and throw things away moved less, and time on task increased for all the students. The room became like a library with whispering instead of talking; it was just so much more comfortable. I am not saying it took care of all of my discipline issues, but it cut them in half, and I do not get any more complaints about student's eyes being tired from reading. I do not think I will ever go back to the harsh ceiling lights again. In fact it hurts my eyes when I have to go to another teacher's room for meetings or to observe; I wonder how they stand it or how I stood it for so long.

A room that is comfortable for my students and me just seems right. I always think back to how I was taught. The teachers I remember—the good ones—made me feel welcomed and comfortable while I was in their room, almost as if I were in their house for an hour. That is what I want my students to think and feel when they come into my class—as if they stepped into my house and feel comfortable enough to share and learn and work together to achieve the goal of further education. (Fig. 6.3)

Fig 6.3

Pre-workshop Trainings   Before attempting workshop, instruct students in several different strategies and techniques to facilitate the process once it is motion. Each group must function independently of each other and without constant teacher guidance. There is a set of skills that students need to understand before they go to the groups. During the first six weeks of the school year, the students and I talk about many of the procedures, routines, and strategies they will follow and use throughout the rest of the school year. The following are some of the areas of concentration although other teachers may emphasize other areas. The beauty of workshop allows for personalization and teachers make it fit their styles of teaching and their students' styles of learning.

Students in the SSR group need to be able to read silently for a period of time and to be able to stop periodically and jot down some notes on sticky notes. This sounds like a simple thing, but after a summer of not reading at all many students need to build their reading stamina. I start the students out slowly with a fifteen minute SSR, keeping an eye on those that fidget toward the end of the time, so I can make adjustments for them and discuss their silent reading during our mini conferences. Writing sticky notes is not difficult either, except what to assign them over. We negotiate that by talking about what good readers do when they read and preserve those skills on an anchor chart.

For writing group (W) students learn about the writing process and the need to save everything they write. It is always an eye-opener for students to learn that the revision process is ongoing and the largest part of writing a paper. Paragraphs, format, and mechanics become integrated as the year progresses and as I teach minilessons or conference with the students. They all find out that form is dictated by function in the end. As with silent reading, students have to be brought slowly up to writing for an entire period. Both are as much tasks of endurance as they are skills, and both take time to reach fulfillment. They are a necessity for workshop to run smoothly. The students will be using these skills for two of the five groups, Writing (W) and Journals (J).

Class novel discussions (CND) are something I work on first with the whole class, modeling how I want the students to ask questions and how I would like them to cite text evidence in their answers. I use *Questioning the Author* (Beck & McKeown, 1998) as a reference when I discuss questions with my students. I use focus questions and follow-up queries and lead everything back to the text for verification. There are other good discussion techniques (including the Junior Great Books Inquiry method, which I used up until a few years ago). The important thing is to find a discussion technique that facilitates students finding the answer, not one that leads them to answer lower level questions.

The independent group (IND) is just that—independent, and they need to be able to function that way. If cooperative learning or some other type of group learning has not already been implemented in the classroom, research some collaborative strategies and find one that works best. Students need to work independently and cooperatively with each other for workshop to have a chance of succeeding. Assigning tasks and rotating those tasks helps the group focus on the assignment. I take time to work on several shorter assignments and/or presentations the first six weeks to prepare students for going about it on their own later. Success breeds competence and further success.

Previously, I described the groundwork that needs to be laid for the Journal group (J) in the section on Writing (W). There are other strategies that need to be taught and modeled to help students work while in this group. In my class the students read (SSR) their self-chosen independent novel for thirty minutes and then write in their journals for ten minutes during the first half of their blocked classes. This is followed by a minilesson and then workshop for the second half of the block. I spend a lot of time modeling journal entries that I write after reading during SSR. Some of my entries are about the novel but many spin off into my experiences and recollections. As I model I talk about what I was thinking as I read and wrote. Some days I role play times where I think of nothing to write about concerning the novel, so I just write what is on my mind that day. I try to model different types of journal entries so students have many options.

Another important part of the Journal group (J) is sharing. I use the journal entries and other assignments during the first six weeks, and we practice at least three or four different share strategies using those entries. I want students to understand they are sharing their writing to get feedback. When they are giving feedback, I want them to understand that it needs to be constructive. I listen to everyone read and hear everyone give feedback at least once to ensure that there are no misunderstandings. This is an important part of the revision process

It takes focused planning and time to get workshop flowing in the classroom. For most of my students this is the first time they have ever experienced this much independence and freedom, and that sometimes leads to undesirable behaviors. I take the time at the beginning of the year to make sure everyone understands exactly what he or she is supposed to accomplish before we set off on workshop. The time spent establishing routines and on instruction in reading and writing at the beginning of the year is well worth my time in fewer headaches the rest of the year.

The first time I group students for workshop, I am more hands-on than I am later in the year. I assign each group a task and then as a class we review the expectations for each group. I do this everyday for the first week so the tasks become familiar to the students, and because as the year progresses the tasks remain consistent—making it easier on me—only the content changes. I spend an equal amount of time with each group answering questions and facilitating. As the year goes on and I am needed less and less in some groups, I gravitate to the discussion group or pull students out for conferences. By the end of the first semester the students know exactly what they need to do and where they need to go; so I am there for clarifications and individual help.

Block or Not   *Because of the time constraints I have to make choices—about the curriculum, about goals, about objectives, about what is best done with the time we have.*

—Linda Rief

I am lucky enough to have a ninety-minute block to work with my students. I say I am lucky because I know what it is like to teach reading and writing for only fifty minutes a day. We changed to the ninety-minute block about six years ago and then I became acquainted with the NJWPT/Abydos. It has been a perfect match.

Ninety minutes gives me time to do many things and still keep the flow and continuity needed for the activities I use. Within the ninety minutes, four groups tackle four different tasks daily. I start each class with twenty-five to thirty minutes of sustained silent reading (SSR) because research shows that daily reading ultimately helps students succeed in their lives.

I follow this with fifteen minutes of journal writing. At the beginning of the year I give the students topics that help them look into their reading and talk about things in their books so they can discover topics and angles to write about. Later in the year I direct them to write about what they read and allow them to choose their focus. Journal writing helps students digest what they read and make personal connections; it is a way for students to review what happened in the novel and what it might mean.

The third task is a minilesson; these take from five to fifteen minutes and are usually either over things with which students struggle in reading and writing, or about new information for them to learn. If it is new information, it is highly probable that I will have subsequent minilessons to cover the same information again in different ways. This is why many of the essentials of NJWPT/Abydos are repeated throughout the year. They help students see how to apply new information to different situations, a strategy that can be utilized by students forever.

The last task is the longest—forty to forty-five minutes—and also the most involved. I reserve the last half of the period for reading/writing workshop. During workshop time students work individually or in groups to complete the different tasks assigned to them. At first I assign the task but towards the end of the year they choose what to work on and in what order. Usually the assignments are of four kinds: reading, discussion, independent work in the novel, and writing from the novel. At times throughout the year and depending on the type of novel we are reading, I add a fifth group of assignments dealing with research. All assignments help to bring out the essential knowledge and skills of reading and writing; they cause students to create connections to the characters and situations in the novel. I spend time with each group during any given class and then settle with one group for more indepth work.

This same schedule may be adapted for a fifty-minute period meeting once a day. I have had to do this on occasion and found that it is not as optimal, but the results are comparable and better than what I was doing before—teaching solely out of textbooks. I found that I could not cover as many novels, so I had to choose the novels carefully based on those I felt had more merit or those that enabled me to teach more skills. Basically I spent two days doing things that only take one day in a block class. I still had SSR and Journal writing everyday, but for less time. The students read for twenty minutes and wrote for ten. A minilesson afterwards used up the rest of the period. The next day the students read and wrote again and then went straight into workshop. At times I had to cut back five minutes on the SSR or eliminate the journal writing if the students were going to be writing during workshop. I also found that with just fifty minutes, I had to assign more outside work. If I had enough novels to assign one to each student, they would read at home so we could concentrate on the assignments in class. If I did not have enough novels, students finish their assignments for homework. Without the block it is a slow process but still well worth the time in the long run.

Works Cited

Anderson, Carl. *How's It Going: A Practical Guide to Conferring with Student Writers.* Portsmouth, NH: Heinemann, 2000.

Aristotle. *Art of Rhetoric.* Cambridge, MA: Harvard University Press, 1932.

Atwell, Nancy. *In the Middle: Writing, Reading, and Learning with Adolescents.* Portsmouth, NH: Heinemann, 1987.

Brock, Paula. *Nudges.* Spring, TX: Absey & Company, Inc., 2004.

Bruffee, Kenneth A. *A Short Course in Writing.* Cambridge, MA: Winthrop, 1972.

Burke, Kenneth. "The Five Key Terms of Dramatism." In *Contemporary Rhetoric: A Conceptual Background with Readings,* W. Ross Winterowd, ed. NY: Harcourt Brace Jovanavich, 1975.

Calkins, Lucy McCormick. *The Art of Teaching Writing.* Portsmouth, NH: Heinemann, 1986.

——— *Lessons From a Child: On the Teaching and Learning of Writing.* Portsmouth, NH: Heinemann, 1983.

Cambourne, Brian. *The Whole Story: Natural Learning and the Acquisition of Literacy in the Classroom.* Auckland, New Zealand: Ashton Scholastic Ltd., 1988.

Carroll, Joyce Armstrong. *Dr. JAC's Reading/Writing Workshop Primer.* Spring, TX: Absey & Company, Inc., 2002.

Carroll, Joyce Armstrong and Edward E. Wilson. *Acts of Teaching.* Englewood, CO: Teacher Idea Press, 1993.

Curtis, Christopher Paul. *The Watsons Go to Birmingham--1963.* NY: Bantam Doubleday Dell Books for Young Readers, 1997.

Elbow, Peter. *Writing with Power.* NY: Oxford University Press, 1973.

——— *Writing without Teachers.* NY: Oxford University Press, 1981.

Feinstein, Sheryl. *Secrets of the Teenage Brain.* San Diego, CA: The Brain Store, 2004.

Gallagher, Kelly. *Deeper Reading Comprehending Challenging Texts, 4-12.* Portland, ME:Stenhouse, 2004.

Gould, June. *The Writer in All of Us.* NY: E. P. Dutton, 1989.

Graves, Donald H. *Writing: Teachers and Children at Work.* Portsmouth, NH: Heinemann, 1983.

Hunt, Kellogg W. "Early Blooming and Late Blooming Syntactic Structures." In *Evaluating Writing. Describing, Measuring, Judging.* Edited by Charles R. Cooper and Lee Odell. 91-106. Urbana, Illinois: NCTE 1977.

Jensen, Eric. *Different Brains, Different Learners: How to Reach the Hard to Reach.* San Diego, CA: The Brain Store, 2000.

Jensen, Eric. *Teaching With the Brain in Mind.* Alexandria, VA: ASCD, 1998.

Krashen, Stephen D. *The Power of Reading: Insights From the Research* 2nd ed. Portsmouth, NH: Libraries Unlimited, 2004.

Lane, Barry. *After the End.* Portsmouth, NH: Heinemann, 1993.

Rief, Linda. *Seeking Diversity: Language Arts with Adolescents.* Portsmouth, NH: Heinemann, 1992.

Romano, Tom. *Clearing The Way: Working with Teenage Writers.* Portsmouth, NH: Heinemann, 1987.

Rosenblatt, Louise M. *The Transactional Theory of Reading and Writing.* NY: MLA, 2004.

Rosenblatt, Louise M. *Literature as Exploration,* 4th ed. NY: MLA, 1983.

Routman, Regie. *Invitations: Changing as Teachers and Learners K-12.* Portsmouth, NH:Heinemann, 1991.

Stillman, Peter R. *Families Writing.* Cincinnati, OH: Writer's Digest Books, 1989.

Tovani, Cris. *Do I Really Have to Teach Reading?* Portland, ME: Stenhouse Publishers, 2004.

Tovani Cris. *I Read It, But I Don't Get It.* Portland, ME: Stenhouse Publishers, 2000.

Zinsser, William. *On Writing Well.* NY: HarperCollins Publishers Inc., 2001.